This timely book describes and explains the American people's alleged hatred of their own branch of government, the U.S. Congress. Intensive focus-group sessions held across the country and a specially designed national survey indicate that much of the negativity is generated by popular perceptions of the processes of governing visible in Congress.

John R. Hibbing and Elizabeth Theiss-Morse argue that, although the public is deeply disturbed by debate, compromise, deliberate pace, the presence of interest groups, and the professionalization of politics, many of these traits are endemic to modern democratic government. Congress is an enemy of the public partially *because* it is so public. Calls for reforms such as term limitations reflect the public's desire to attack these disliked features. Acknowledging the need for some reforms to be taken more seriously, the authors conclude that the public's unwitting desire to reform democracy out of a democratic legislature is a cure more dangerous than the disease.

CONGRESS AS PUBLIC ENEMY

Cambridge Studies in Political Psychology and Public Opinion

General Editors

James H. Kuklinski and Robert S. Wyer, Jr.
University of Illinois, Urbana-Champaign

Editorial Board

Stanley Feldman, *State University of New York,*
Stony Brook
Roger D. Masters, *Dartmouth College*
William J. McGuire, *Yale University*
Norbert Schwarz, *Zentrum für Umfragen, Methoden*
und Analysen ZUMA, Mannheim, FRG
David O. Sears, *University of California, Los Angeles*
Paul M. Sniderman, *Stanford University and Survey*
Research Center, University of California, Berkeley
James A. Stimson, *University of Minnesota*

This series has been established in recognition of the growing sophistication in the resurgence of interest in political psychology and the study of public opinion. Its focus ranges from the kinds of mental processes that people employ when they think about democratic processes and make political choices to the nature and consequences of macro-level public opinion.

Some of the works draw on developments in cognitive and social psychology, and relevant areas of philosophy. Appropriate subjects include the use of heuristics, the role of core values and moral principles in political reasoning, the effects of expertise and sophistication, the roles of affect and emotion, and the nature of cognition and information processing. The emphasis is on systematic and rigorous empirical analysis, and a wide range of methodologies are appropriate: traditional surveys, experimental surveys, laboratory experiments, focus groups, in-depth interviews, as well as others. These empirically oriented studies also consider normative implications for democratic politics generally.

Politics, not psychology, is the primary focus, and it is expected that most works will deal with mass publics and democratic politics, although work on nondemocratic publics is not excluded. Other works will examine traditional topics in public opinion research, as well as contribute to the growing literature on aggregate opinion and its role in democratic societies.

Other books in the series

CONGRESS AS PUBLIC ENEMY

Public attitudes toward
American political institutions

JOHN R. HIBBING
University of Nebraska, Lincoln

ELIZABETH THEISS-MORSE
University of Nebraska, Lincoln

CAMBRIDGE
UNIVERSITY PRESS

Published by the Press Syndicate of the University of Cambridge
The Pitt Building, Trumpington Street, Cambridge CB2 1RP
40 West 20th Street, New York, NY 10011-4211, USA
10 Stamford Road, Oakleigh, Melbourne 3166, Australia

© Cambridge University Press 1995

First published 1995

Printed in the United States of America

Library of Congress Cataloging-in-Publication Data
Hibbing, John R.
Congress as public enemy: public attitudes toward American
political institutions / John R. Hibbing, Elizabeth Theiss-Morse.
p.   cm. – (Cambridge studies in political psychology and

public opinion)
Includes bibliographical references and index.
ISBN 0-521-48299-2 (hc). – ISBN 0-521-48336-0 (pbk.)
1. United States. Congress – Public opinion.   2. United States.
Congress – Reform.   3. Public opinion – United States.   I. Theiss-
Morse, Elizabeth.   II. Title.   III. Series.
JK1041.H53   1995
328.7307 – dc20   95-3513
                                         CIP

A catalog record for this book is available from the British Library.

ISBN 0-521-48299-2 hardback
ISBN 0-521-48336-0 paperback

To the buddies: Michael, Matthew, and Anthony
And to the folks: Fred and Sue Theiss

Contents

Figures

Tables

Preface

In the space of a few weeks during the summer of 1992 we attended two very different meetings dealing with the perceived problems of Congress and the overall political system. Participants at the first meeting were congressional staffers, residents of Washington think tanks, employees of the Congressional Research Service, and university professors specializing in the study of Congress. The prevailing sentiment of this group was that while the public's perceptions of congressional inadequacies could not be ignored, these perceptions were wholly inaccurate and potentially dangerous. At one point, someone even suggested that more needed to be done to "insulate" Congress from the public. This comment drew murmurs of approval from others in the room. Much of the rest of the discussion centered around ideas such as strengthening the powers of party leaders, modifying some of the internal rules of the Senate (such as those dealing with holds – the norm allowing senators to delay voting on a bill), and perhaps altering the jurisdiction of House committees.

The second group consisted of residents of a small midwestern town. None of them had ever worked for Congress; many had never even been to Washington. They were brought together to determine what ordinary people saw as causes of and solutions to the problems of Congress and our political system. The answers proposed by these people were quite different from those of the congressional specialists. The nonspecialists believed members of Congress to be haughty, pampered, and out of touch. They disliked the committee system, they felt Congress was too partisan, and they were in the mood for serious reform. They were not interested in minor tinkering with the rules, they had difficulty fathoming how Congress could be more insulated than it was already, and they certainly were not excited by the prospects of giving additional power to congressional power brokers, whether party or committee bosses. Their preferred reform agenda was, to say the least, quite a bit different from that of the congressional insiders with whom we had met earlier. Term limits, abolishing most staff positions, eliminating committees, and removing perquisites of office were all mentioned frequently.

The contrast between the two groups was jarring but revealing. The notion that a political body based on representation could improve by insulating itself from the people it is supposed to represent is puzzling and may indicate that it is possible for analysts to get too close to what they are analyzing. Those familiar with the scientific process are acutely aware of the fact that the act of observation can alter that which is being observed; this is widely known as the Hawthorne Effect. Much less discussed, unfortunately, is that the act of observation can also alter the observer. In fact, this is so little discussed that it has not been given a name; thus, we humbly dub it the John and Beth Effect. Congressional insiders would do well to remember this effect.

Equally puzzling is the unrefined populist pining of so many citizens. They seem to expect Congress, magically, to mold sometimes bitterly divided public opinion into coherent and effective public policy without debate, disagreement, or compromise. They seem to expect Congress to oversee the mammoth federal executive branch, service the diverse demands of constituents, and make good law in the technologically complex and confusing postindustrial era, all with minimal staff, support, division of labor, and compensation. And they seem to believe that whenever Congress listens to the arguments of a political party or an interest group it has done something unspeakably evil.

Congressional insiders and ordinary people are both off base, we argue, and the academic social-science community has been of remarkably little assistance in illuminating the real problems. We hear much talk these days of a "new institutionalism" in the study of American politics. Unfortunately, this new institutionalism is unduly focused on esoteric internal rules and edifices. As the public exudes a new populism, oblivious academics are hypnotized by a recycled, insider institutionalism. People need to be brought into the equation, but academic research is ill-equipped on this count as well. The study of public opinion has its own unfortunate bias, which runs toward survey work on voting behavior. Broader issues such as how the (voting *and* nonvoting) public relates to its political system have been given short shrift, as have research strategies more imaginative than machine-gunning closed-ended questions over the telephone. The study of political institutions and ordinary people must be united. It is, after all, the combination of institutions and people that forms a polity.

In this book, we present the results of our research on the manner in which ordinary people relate to the major political institutions of the United States government. We have not eschewed survey research, but we have pursued what seems to us to be a more suitably balanced approach. Our findings are based on more than 1,400 thirty-minute telephone interviews with a nationwide sample of voting-age residents, but also on eight two-hour focus-group sessions conducted at locales across the country and consisting of approximately ten participants each. These independent data bases should allow us to provide the most complete analysis available of the public's perceptions of political institutions.

Our primary focus is on the Congress – the first branch, the people's branch. Congress is at the center of government and, therefore, at the center of the unrest with government that is currently so pervasive in the United States. Indeed, our interest in this topic was fanned by what seemed in the early 1990s to be a spreading and deepening intensity of unrest with Congress. Many observers did not know what to make of this unrest. Why, when, and from where did it come? At one level we hope that by analyzing various kinds of data we will be able to explain recent unrest with Congress, an unrest that likely fed into the momentous shift in the partisan control of Congress in 1994.

But at a deeper level, we hope to present a more theoretical approach to public attitudes toward political institutions. We do not confine ourselves to questions concerning one institution during one period of time; rather, we place recent attitudes toward Congress in broader perspective. We believe part of the reason observers are befuddled by public attitudes of the day is the dearth of general theoretical work on public attitudes themselves. Another part of the problem is the unsatisfactory nature of existing data, consisting as they do of little more than poorly worded, sporadically asked survey questions. In this project, we hope to unite improved data with quality theorizing on a topic of crucial importance to the governing process.

Our aim is not to antagonize unnecessarily congressional insiders or Congress bashers, new institutionalists or students of public opinion. Rather, we wish to urge on all of the above a new appreciation of public attitudes toward institutions, a new realization of the dangers of being either overly defensive or overly critical of the status quo, and a new recognition both that institutions can matter for reasons other than their effect on substantive policy and that public opinion can matter for reasons other than the way it shapes vote choice.

We write these words as bodies continue to be pulled from the remains of the federal building in Oklahoma City. That structure's tragic bombing was apparently the product of an intense hatred of the U.S. government, and this alleged motivation has therefore stimulated widespread discussion of the possibility that general societal negativity and, especially, the sometimes inflammatory rhetoric present in much modern public debate could have played a contributing role. Politicians such as President Clinton and House Speaker Gingrich have traded comments on the issue, as have columnists such as E. J. Dionne, Jr., and George Will. We do not pretend to know the extent to which the actions of a lunatic fringe may be connected to more mainstream attitudes toward the merits of the U.S. government, but we do know that the bombing is a gut-wrenching reminder of the need to learn more about how all kinds of people relate to their government and its institutions. As will be evident in the pages that follow, we believe a major problem with this relationship, as currently constituted, is the lack of public appreciation of the extent to which opinion is split on most issues and of the consequent need to tolerate policies and procedures we might not like. The Oklahoma City bombing is a sobering reminder of what happens when intolerance of government gets out of hand, and it is this very intolerance of democratic government that is the topic of our book.

The pages that follow constitute the culmination of a difficult but enjoyable project. We have received much help along the way. The project's main source of financial assistance was the National Science Foundation (SES-91-22733). We deeply appreciate the help of Frank Scioli, Jim Campbell, and the NSF. Secondary financial support came from the University of Nebraska Foundation Fund for Research on the U.S. Congress. The Bureau of Sociological Research at the University of Nebraska performed the telephone interviews with its usual high degree of professionalism. We thank Cheryl Yorges, T. Wayne Osgood, and their fine team. The focus-group sessions would have been immensely more difficult save for the untiring coordinating efforts of Cynthia Berreau. We also thank Mark Watts from the University of Minnesota, Sara Keith from Syracuse University, and Beth Nelson, Dan Cox, and Christine Pappas from the University of Nebraska for their help. Special thanks go to Rick Wilson for help on the Houston sessions and to Amy Fried for help on the New York sessions. We appreciate the extremely helpful comments of Richard Brody, James Kuklinski, Bruce Oppenheimer, and Samuel C. Patterson, and the invaluable editorial assistance of Alex Holzman. Finally, we thank our families for their assistance and patience during the long, long journey from the first draft of the grant proposal to a completed book.

CONGRESS AS PUBLIC ENEMY

I

Introduction:
What is wrong with
the American political system?

The voices of citizens matter in a democracy, but understanding what these voices are truly saying is difficult. We know that the American public in the 1990s holds the political system, and the institutions composing it, in astonishingly low regard. We also know that people, outside of a temporary honeymoon with the 104th Congress and its new partisan majority, are especially disgusted with Congress. The reason for these negative feelings is much less clear. If we are to understand what citizens are saying, however, we must determine what lies behind their antipathy. We pursue this task in the pages that follow. Our primary thesis is that dissatisfaction with the political system and especially Congress is due in no small part to public perceptions of the *processes* involved. As will become apparent, some aspects of these allegedly flawed governing processes are of the sort that could be improved through the adoption of certain political reforms, but other aspects are endemic to open democratic government. That the people of the United States, a country often viewed as the initiator of modern democratic government, have an aversion to democratic processes may sound absurd to many, and perhaps obvious to a few, but we ask for patience as we develop the evidence and logic behind this contention and as we append the necessary caveats and qualifications.

The public's negativity toward the political system and Congress has reached the saturation point. It pours forth with only the slightest provocation and has been duly recorded by countless political observers. In fact, these sentiments have been so much a part of the recent scene that only the briefest sampling is needed here. The title and first few paragraphs of a 1991 *Washington Post* article include these words and phrases: "an electorate ready to revolt," "anger," "frustration," "crisis of confidence," a political system "under indictment," "crisis of confidence" (again), "disaffection," "anxiety," "decline of confidence" (for variety), "disillusionment," "government off track," "frustrations," and "further frustrations" (for good measure) (Balz & Morin, 1991).

The *Post* is hardly alone. A feature article in the *Atlantic Monthly* begins by noting that "from the term-limitation movement to the rise of Ross Perot, the signs of discontent with the political status quo are everywhere" (Lind, 1992). The Institute of Governmental Studies at the University of California, Berkeley, hosted a workshop in 1992 organized around the question, "What is Wrong with American Political Institutions?" The institute's director, Nelson Polsby, begins his recap of the workshop by noting the "rising tide of dissatisfaction with the functioning of the American political system" (1991: 1). Alan Ehrenhalt writes that "it is hard to find anyone in America these days who does not believe that something has gone wrong with the country's political system. Anger and frustration seem to spill out the moment politics comes up in casual conversation" (1991: xviii).

The title of E. J. Dionne, Jr.'s book on the topic is *Why Americans Hate Politics* (1991). The widely cited report of the Kettering Foundation sees the situation as so bleak that "the challenge before us today is to reconnect citizens and politics – to find a place for citizens in the political process" (1991). *Congressional Quarterly Weekly Report*, a publication not usually given to hyperbole, refers to "tidal waves of discontent" (Hook, 1990: 2473). And *Time* reports that the major message being sent by the people these days is "a blunt and resounding 'no'! No to the lies and intrigues of Washington, no to spending by politicians who can't be trusted with the public's dollars, no to a money greased political system dedicated to self-preservation rather than leadership" (Gibbs, 1990: 32).

While it is difficult to locate a portion of the political system currently held in high esteem, it is not difficult to locate the focal point of the alleged public unrest. It is, fittingly, the first branch of government, the U.S. Congress. The initial report of the joint American Enterprise Institute and Brookings Institution effort to renew Congress begins by stating simply: "Make no mistake about it: Congress is in trouble" (1992: 2). We are told that people believe Congress is the broken branch, that it is an embattled institution (Ehrenhalt, 1992), that its approval rating among the public is at an all-time low (*Public Perspective*, 1992: 86–87), that Congress faces "a wave of public criticism that is unprecedented in recent memory" (Uslaner, 1992: 1), and that "the public hates Congress" (Broder & Morin, 1994). "That the people are angry at Congress is abundantly clear," writes James J. Kirkpatrick (1992: 19).

To be sure, support for Congress increased in the early months of 1995. The 1994 midterm election radically changed the partisan makeup of Congress, and changed the majority party in the House of Representatives for the first time in forty years. The public's willingness to give the new regime a decent chance, combined with that regime's own rhetoric about enacting major changes in a short, one-hundred-day period, led to a predictable upsurge in public support for Congress. Tellingly, however, virtually no one expected this situation to last. Instead, it was widely anticipated that before long, approval ratings for Congress would return to the dismal levels evident in the early 1990s.

Is this sense of gloom produced solely by inordinate attention to the views of uninformed populist agitators? Hardly. Thomas E. Mann, director of governmental studies at Brookings, believes the legitimacy of the institution of Congress has been eroded, "especially within the political class" (Cohen, 1992: 119). Members of Congress themselves tend to be the most critical (see, for example, Craig, 1993: chapter 5) and those members who have already left Congress are often the most caustic of all (see, for example, Hibbing, 1982). Dennis Hertel (D.-Mich.) retired from the House in 1992, saying he was "angry and frustrated with Congress." Lawrence Coughlin (R.-Penn.) also retired in 1992, citing a "demeaned" Congress. Their fellow retiree, Edward Feighan (D.-Ohio), explained his decision by referring to "a small group of partisan extremists who have set out to destroy the institution" (all quoted in Katz, 1992). Thus, criticisms are not being made solely out of a desire to improve chances in the next election campaign (what Fenno, 1975, refers to as running for Congress by running against Congress).

It is now common practice, both for those retiring from Congress and for those staying, to complain about the hectic pace, the difficulty of passing legislation, the lack of comity among members, shrill demands from the people, the demanding interest groups, the intrusive media, and the byzantine, balkanized legislative process (for the complaints of sitting members, see the hearings of the Joint Committee on the Organization of Congress, 1993). Alas, House Republicans' 1995 success in eliminating three minor committees and a few dozen subcommittees was hardly sufficient to alter these perceptions. Perhaps the most jarring statement on the plight of Congress came when William Gray (D.-Penn.), who held one of the more powerful positions in the House as majority whip, explained his decision to leave Congress by noting that he wanted to make a difference in society. It used to be that people entered Congress because they wanted to make a difference; now it appears that some leave for the same reason.

So, virtually everyone – insiders and outsiders alike – seems to be upset with our national political institutions and particularly with Congress. The unrest may appear most intense outside the beltway, but many Washingtonians also are sincerely disappointed with the current functioning of the political system. Discontent seems ubiquitous. Indeed, as we were writing this book, people would occasionally ask us what we were doing. Our answer, that we were attempting to determine what the public really thought about Congress and the other political institutions, nearly always drew a reaction something like this: "Why do you need to study that? Everyone knows people hate Congress and politics. What more needs to be said?"

It will come as no surprise that we believe much more needs to be said, largely because – and this is a surprise – so little has been said to date. Plenty of recorded thoughts are relevant, and we will mention many of these, but no one has adequately tackled the nature and reasons for public disaffection. More specifically, it is our belief that the best approach to understanding public dissatisfaction with the political system is to analyze public reactions to key parts of that system; namely, institutions. Moreover, we believe that an appreciation of the public's attitudes toward these individual institutions is important in and of itself. We need to know, for example, what the public thinks about Congress and why. It is not the case that everybody "hates" Congress. Hate is neither a very specific nor, as we shall argue, a very accurate term in this context. Further, Congress and the other political institutions are structurally and functionally multifaceted, and people, as it turns out, vary widely in their perceptions of and attitudes toward the different parts both of Congress and of the rest of the political system, often hating some parts while feeling a good deal less hostile toward others.

Obtaining an accurate fix on people's attitudes toward diverse components of diverse political institutions is not a well-mapped task. Accordingly, previous research has adopted numerous approaches. Many of these, particularly those of a more focused (on a single institution) and technical bent, will be described in the next chapter. In the remainder of this chapter, we are thus free to summarize several more general and often more impressionistic accounts of the public's problems with the entire political system. A primary motivation in enumerating these is to communicate the diversity of explanations for why people allegedly despise their own political system.

We argue that major reasons for the disparate and speculative nature of these explanations are the absence of good data and good theory pertaining to public attitudes toward political institutions. Survey questions on political institutions have usually been superficial, poorly worded, posed sporadically, or accompanied by inadequate or nonexistent background questions. Existing theory is no better than existing data. The main theoretical insight available to organize expectations and findings pertaining to public perceptions of political institutions is the distinction between specific support (support for particular decisions or policies, for example) and more diffuse support (that not contingent

4

upon recent events). This insight, we argue, is somewhat misleading; but even if it were not, it hardly constitutes an appropriate theoretical framework for a task as important as putting into perspective the public's views of core governmental structures.

Our goal is, first, to provide suitable data on public perceptions of and attitudes toward Congress and the other federal political institutions. We adopt an institutionally oriented approach in which data are obtained on public attitudes toward individual political institutions rather than on the political system as a whole. Second, using data unique to each institution, we will then construct a more complete theory of popular political support in the United States. This theory, in turn, should allow more meaningful interpretations of the current "crisis of confidence" in American political institutions. Absent the needed theory and data, interpretations of the current unrest are likely to be all over the map – and this is just what we discover to be the case.

WHY THE CRISIS OF CONFIDENCE IN THE POLITICAL SYSTEM?

Attention to the current crisis of confidence has become so widespread that suggested explanations run rampant. The range of these general explanations is practically unlimited, with many of them being contradictory or at least noncumulative. They often lack systematic evidence. Nonetheless, these explanations on occasion have a ring of truth that should not be ignored. We provide a brief summary of the key tenets of several explanations, thus helping set the stage for our own analysis. The explanations we examine differ in terms of what the perceived problem is and who or what is the cause of it. Are citizens themselves to blame? Has the government lost touch with the electorate? Have politicians lost all credibility? Is the political system itself simply not working anymore? We try to gain a handle on explanations of public unrest by focusing on four targets of blame: politicians and the media, government policies, political processes, and the citizens themselves.

Politicians and the media

Some explanations of the current crisis of confidence point the finger of blame both at politicians (primarily, it is important to note, simply for being politicians) and also at the media (for inflaming negative feelings in the general public). Disagreement exists, however, over which politicians are to blame, over how long people have been disgusted, and over the precise role the media play in all of this.

First, some people argue that the problem is with politicians in general, as is evident in the fact that citizens have disliked them almost forever. Evidence supporting this view can be found easily. Historically, people have liked to dislike politicians, and especially members of Congress. Enduring public derision is part of the politician's job, and negative comments about Congress and politicians have been made throughout U.S. history. Survey data also support this view. For example, Gallup data indicate that in the mid- and late 1940s, few people believed Congress was doing a good job (usually around 15 to 25 percent of respondents). Data from the early 1950s show that approximately 70 percent of survey respondents said that term limits for members of Congress were a good idea, which very closely matches public support for term limits when the issue exploded on the scene in the late 1980s (see Ladd, 1990).

If people have historically disliked politicians, according to this view, then the current lack of confidence is in many ways simply a continuation of a historical trend. What has changed, however, is the tone with which the media cover politics and politicians. The media persistently and eagerly broadcast every misstep by every member of Congress and publicize every negative poll result. This coverage may eventually have convinced the public that politicians really are much worse than in earlier times and that the political system itself is in need of reform. Glenn Parker laments that "congressional unpopularity is often treated by the mass media and political observers as a malady in desperate need of remedy," when in fact "we should expect congressional performance to receive low marks" (1981: 32). The implication is that, while lack of public esteem for politics and politicians may not be something we can ignore, we certainly should not overreact to chronic disappointments with the understandable failure of politicians to please everyone all the time. And the negative media coverage has not changed people's basic support for the political system. The public gives the core constitutional design high marks and thinks that the U.S. system of government is basically sound (Roper, February 1981 polls, cited in Lipset & Schneider, 1987: 385).

A related explanation also includes politicians and the media, but puts a different spin on the current unrest. People who subscribe to this view say that the problem, a recent one, is the widespread decline in confidence in leaders of a wide variety of institutions, only some of which are political. This decline was caused, perhaps, by events such as the Vietnam War, but more likely by the media's portrayal of the inability of institutional leaders to handle important problems facing the nation.

According to this explanation, something fundamental did in fact change in recent years, thereby causing a general loss of public faith in America's leaders whether they be in government, medicine, the military, higher education, business, labor, organized religion, or the media. The evidence accumulated by proponents of this view, including Lipset and Schneider (1987) and Harris (1987), is impressive in many ways. Lipset and Schneider, for example, rely on survey questions that asked people about their confidence in the leaders of ten "institutions" ranging from medicine to labor to political institutions. As will be seen in more detail in Chapter 2, they find that confidence in these leaders has indeed taken a nosedive since the mid 1960s, dropping from an average of 47 percent to 27 percent between 1967 and 1971 (1987: 50). Part of this decline was due to decreased confidence in leaders of political institutions, including the leaders of Congress (falling from 41 to 19 percent), of the executive branch (dropping from 37 to 23 percent), and of the Supreme Court (dropping from 40 to 23 percent). But confidence in all but two nongovernmental institutions fell a strikingly similar amount.

What is the cause of this decline in confidence? Since dissatisfaction was not targeted solely at the leaders of political institutions, the search for causes of the decline naturally is directed toward nonpolitical explanations. Lipset and Schneider, after considering several possibilities, in the end cite media presentations of the inability of institutions such as the firm, the government, the family, and the professions to handle problems like race relations, the Vietnam War, the economy, and the social climate as the cause of the broad-based disillusionment. So leaders of political institutions are culpable, but no more than other societal leaders (1987: 399–406).

Regardless of the precise argument made, proponents of these explanations see some kind of interaction between politicians and the media's reportage of politicians' actions as the key to understanding unrest. Members of the media play a role by emphasizing the bad and playing down the good, while politicians play a role by providing plenty of raw material for the media.

Government policies

A second type of explanation, as popular as the first, holds that the government has increasingly pursued policies discordant with the public's wishes. The public reacts not only by feeling dissatisfied about policy options, but also by feeling distrustful of the government. William Gamson says distrust of the government arises out of "the nature of the decisions made and the satisfaction or dissatisfaction with them" (1968: 178). But proponents of this view are fundamentally at odds over whether the government is too centrist or too extremist in its policies.

Arthur Miller (1974), for example, argues that the decreased trust people feel toward government stems from their perception that neither major party represents their policy views. When people feel strongly about a particular policy yet can find no party that reflects their view, they become disaffected with the two parties and with the political system itself. A Democrat may, in the past, have disliked the policy stands of the Republican party, but at least the Democratic party closely approximated his or her policy stands. Beginning in the late 1960s, however, as the electorate polarized, this same person came to see no viable alternative in either party, thereby losing trust in government itself. The parties were too similar and centrist at a time when the public held more extreme views on many political issues. Government policies, in essence, were too middle-of-the-road.

Jack Citrin, in his rejoinder to Miller, questions the implications of decreased trust in the political system, but says that he "accepts Miller's main conclusion that *policy-related* discontent is a source of political cynicism" (1974: 974; our emphasis). He further argues, however, that this dissatisfaction then becomes focused on incumbents who have made the policies rather than on the political system and its values. He also does not accept Miller's argument that the government needs to pursue more extremist policies. He·instead makes the point that, regardless of the ideological orientation of particular policies, people may become cynical because government officials promise too much and deliver too little.

E. J. Dionne, Jr., in his influential book *Why Americans Hate Politics*, also argues that the public is upset because of undesirable government policies; but, in direct contradiction to Miller, Dionne believes people think the policy options are too extremist. According to Dionne, Americans' hatred of politics stems from the spokespersons of the major political parties and the major ideologies in the United States being too extreme and dichotomous in their views, and therefore out of step with the vast majority of Americans, who are basically centrists at heart. The present ideological and party apparatus in the United States pushes us toward negative campaigning, banalities, artificially dichotomous choices, and unnecessary polarization. Both the Left and the Right are busy fighting their own internecine battles, and the public is left out. The two major parties (Democratic and Republican) and the two major ideologies (liberalism and conservatism) simply fail to speak for modern America, according to this view.

"What is required to end America's hatred of politics is an organizing idea that simultaneously accepts the efficiencies of markets and the importance of a vigorous public life" (Dionne, 1991: 354). Dionne's view of the present situation is obviously that liberals have been too slow to appreciate the benefits of the market, while conservatives have been too slow to recognize that the effects of the market need to be softened by

8

some sort of benevolent public presence. As a result, according to Dionne, the legacy of the past thirty years is "a polarized politics that highlights symbolic issues, short-circuits genuine political debate, [and] gives discontent few real outlets" (1991: 323).

Morris Fiorina also believes people are often frustrated by the need to make choices between what he terms "San Francisco Democrats," whom many perceive to be the party of "minorities, gay rights activists, radical feminists, and peaceniks," and "Reagan Republicans," the party of "fundamentalists, bigots, pro-life activists, and chicken-hawks" (1992: 74). Craving something in between, the public acts in ways that divide government control between these two undesired extremes.

Whether government policies are too extremist, as Dionne and Fiorina argue, or too centrist, as Miller argues was true in the late 1960s, the public is seen as being less than happy with the policy options being offered by the government and opposition, and therefore as disaffected with politics. If the government could better represent the policy interests of the American people, then trust in government would increase and the people would once again like politics.

Public shut out of the political process

A third and rarer view argues that public dissatisfaction and discontent stem from the public's sense that it is shut out of the political process. Yet there are disagreements over what has led to the perceived exclusion of citizens from the public sphere. One explanation points to the "Washington system" and another to the increased professionalization and institutionalization of Congress.

According to the widely cited Kettering Foundation Report, issued in 1991, the American people are dissatisfied because they have been shut out of the political process by Washington insiders, careerist politicians, and special interests who now seem to control the political system itself. The basic message of the report is that the American public, far from being apathetic or uninterested in politics, is actually eager to get involved. Unfortunately, the public is estranged from the political system. The governing system is perceived to be big, alien, and out of their control.

Is this a recent phenomenon? The answer to this question is unclear, although evidence from several focus-group sessions around the country indicates that participants in the Kettering study felt that the political process had moved away from ordinary citizens. Many participants stressed the role of political action committees (PACs), extremists, special interests, and careerist politicians, so presumably the increased visibility of these entities is a factor. Another possibility is that the increased population in the United States and the growth in the size of the government have made people feel as if no one is listening to them anymore. The key point, however, is that according to this view the political process has, for some largely unspecified reason, spun out of the control of ordinary citizens and become the servant of nefarious special interests. People try to be contributing, politically involved citizens, but believe they have been shut out of the political process due to the nature of the system itself. According to this view, the political process has failed us.

An alternative and in some ways complementary explanation holds that people have been shut out of the system by the increased professionalization of politicians and institutionalization of Congress. Congress has become a world unto itself, a world the public does not like. Alan Ehrenhalt, author of *The United States of Ambition*, believes the main source of the problem in the minds of the public is the absence of citizen-politicians. In their place we find political offices dominated by "a careerist elite whose lifetime political preoccupation has separated them from most people" (1991: xx). Of course professional politicians are only part of a professionalized political system.

In Nelson Polsby's (1968) well-known formulation, professionalization, or institutionalization as it is sometimes called, consists of increasing complexity, boundedness, and devotion to standard operating procedures. In an institutionalized Congress, members stay longer, leaders are increasingly required to serve a long apprenticeship period within the Congress (unlike Henry Clay, who was made Speaker of the House the first day he served), the number of staff assistants has increased, committees have more clout and permanence, norms and rules of the game are more apparent, and the existence of elaborate congressional infrastructures, consisting of eateries, barbershops, and support agencies, all mushroomed. All this is a far cry from the lonely citizen-legislator who served to promote the commonweal and did not benefit from six-figure salaries, perquisites, special parking places, scores of doting staffers, and stable and lengthy career paths. Most citizens of today are not at all fond of either professional politicians or big, professional political institutions, and both contribute to a hatred of politics.[1]

According to these views, the public's disaffection is due to the polit-

---

1 But Ehrenhalt argues persuasively that the problem in actuality is not that politicians have lost touch with the American people, because we see "legislators dashing home every weekend for luncheons and forums and town meetings," "members taking polls on every conceivable subject and then shrinking from any action that fails to command at least 51 percent approval," and "legislators mired in weeks of embarrassing deadlock because they fear the electoral consequences of either reducing public services or imposing the taxes those services require" (1991: xiii–xiv). It is possible to see the members of Congress as being too close to the people (see also Will, 1992).

ical process itself. People believe that the way politics is currently run ignores the common person. Only Washington denizens such as ossified members of Congress and special-interest puppets have a say in what is going on in the country, and the public is increasingly kept out of the political process.

Citizens

Finally, it can be argued that while the current problem with government is its inability to get anything done, the real blame does not fall on politicians, policies, or the political process. Rather, the blame actually falls on citizens themselves, who often make contradictory and unreasonable demands while not doing what it takes to fix the perceived problems. The evidence supporting such an argument is abundant. People generally do not pay much attention to politics, and they participate irregularly if at all. Many people do not know the names of their members of Congress and are usually unable to recall a single position taken by a member on a substantive policy matter (see Miller & Stokes, 1963). Barely half of the eligible electorate votes, even in presidential elections, and turnout in midterm, local, and primary elections is substantially lower. People seem much more willing to complain than to try to correct the problems.

Moreover, it often seems as though the demands made by the public are unrealistic. Citizens decry pork-barrel politics in general but are delighted when their own representative is successful in playing the game. They hate negative campaigning but are taken in by it. They complain because politicians do not listen to them and in practically the same breath complain that politicians are captives of polls and lack the backbone required to demonstrate true leadership. People become angry with politicians for not balancing the budget but do not want to pay the price in higher taxes, reduced services, or both, to do so. If people would take their citizen responsibilities seriously and be reasonable, according to this view, then many of the problems facing the nation today could more readily be solved by politicians who, after all, are supposed to be responsive to public desires.

PROBLEMS WITH EXISTING THEORIES

To be sure, the explanations presented are caricatures, and many of the works we have associated with them are richer and do a better job of acknowledging the validity of other explanations than is suggested by our brief discussion. Still, we think a fair reading of recent literature and commentary does reveal that the crux of the problem is seen quite differently by different people. It is obvious that the thrust of various explanations is inconsistent with, perhaps contradictory to, at least some of the others. What, then, can we conclude about public disgust toward politics? Not a great deal.

That these explanations are all over the board points to two major problems faced by anyone trying to understand people's attitudes toward the political system. First, the data available on these attitudes are limited at best. We will discuss problems with data more thoroughly in Chapter 2. For now, suffice it to say that popular explanations of public disgust are based on less than exemplary data; usually some combination of a casual reading of historical trends, sporadic and often limited survey data, unsystematic focus-group responses, and varied experiences with and within the current political system constitute the evidence collected to support these explanations. Making progress in understanding public disaffection depends on having better data.

Second, we also need better theory to guide research on public attitudes toward the political system, and this point deserves to be addressed immediately. Analysts turning to political science in hopes of finding a theoretical framework for understanding the current public unrest must be sorely disappointed by what they find, or rather do not find. The only theory in political science that directly addresses political-system support is found in the work of David Easton (1965a,b). Easton envisions a political system with inputs in the form of demands and support. The system processes these demands and support in a fashion unspecified by the theory, with the result being policy outputs. These outputs, in turn, affect subsequent demands and support via a feedback loop.

Problems with diffuse and specific support

In discussing support as an input (in truth, support is not an input at all but a trait that can condition how inputs are handled), Easton draws a distinction between diffuse and specific support. This distinction has become the essence of the theoretical base for research on attitudes toward the political system. Diffuse support is support "that continues independently of the specific rewards which the member [of the polity] may feel he obtains from belonging to the system" (1965a: 125). Specific support, as might be expected, is "a return for the specific benefits and advantages that members of a system experience as part of their membership. It represents or reflects the satisfaction a member feels when he perceives his demands as having been met" (1965a: 125).

The distinction between diffuse and specific support raises some serious concerns. First, as Craig argues, Easton's theoretical distinction between the two types of support is tautological and therefore impossible to test and falsify:

> The difficulty arises because Easton's argument is tautological in suggesting that (1) any measure of affect found to covary with short-term performance satisfactions cannot, by definition, be diffuse support . . . and that, conversely, (2) any loss of affect leading to mass mobilization and demands for systemic change cannot, by definition, be specific support. . . . both orientations are defined largely in terms of their hypothesized antecedents and consequences, such that exceptions can be interpreted only as the product of inferior methodology. (1993: 9)

Without being able to test the implications of Easton's theory, the distinction between diffuse and specific support does little to increase our understanding of public unrest.

Second, we are troubled by Easton's definitions of these two kinds of support. Specific support, according to usual usage, arises when people like the political system only because they are happy with the specific outputs it has provided. Our view is that such highly conditional, transient support is not really support at all but merely a temporary satisfaction with a recent decision or condition. Easton seemed to recognize as much when, in a reconsideration of the concept of support, he acknowledges that "specific support is a response to the authorities; it is only indirectly relevant, if at all, to the input of support for the regime" (1975: 437). Thus, we question whether specific support is really support at all.

What Easton calls diffuse support is closer to traditional notions of support, reaching deeper than the superficial and ephemeral reactions to particular outputs. Yet, as we see the situation, support, including diffuse support, is not immutable since it can be affected by particular outputs, scandals, and conditions. Just as party identification has come to be viewed by some as a "running tally" (Fiorina, 1981) of favorable and unfavorable features people associate with the parties, support for the political system should be viewed as a running tally of favorable and unfavorable features people associate with the system. Support of any kind is by definition more than reactions to any single output or action. Rather it is the combination of personal predispositions and remembered events. The extent to which support is influenced by particular events and outputs is an empirical issue of the utmost importance and one we hope to explicate.

Inattention to process

An important and unfortunate by-product of Easton's theoretical approach is that attention is directed toward outputs and away from processes. We argue that people's support for the political system is influenced at least as much by the processes employed in the political system as by the particular outputs emanating from the process. Policy is important, but the public's perceptions of how that policy was arrived at also matters. Unrest with Congress after the Anita Hill–Clarence Thomas hearings was not centered on the decision itself, but on the process leading to that decision: the way things looked; the way the hearings were run and how they unfolded; and the institution's structures, rules, and norms.

To take a slightly less well-remembered incident, dissatisfaction with Congress appeared to intensify during the fall of 1990 when then-president Bush and the leaders of Congress were attempting to negotiate an agreement on deficit reduction. The actual decision by both the president and the Congress resulted in what at the time was the most serious deficit-reduction attempt in well over a decade, but the substance was not the key issue in the minds of the public. People were angry at the haggling, the bargaining, the delays, and the visible politicking that was involved. The federal government was technically out of funds for a period of time, and the entire scene surrounding the economic summit and subsequent congressional consideration of the plan was played out in the open more than is usually the case. The public found all this quite distasteful. Partisan politics was obviously at work; so was compromise and deal making. Reaction was strongly negative, and confidence in our institutions of government and the overall system was reduced.

We contend that Easton ignores an important element contributing to or detracting from system support: the processes employed within that system. What do we mean by processes? In many respects, public concern with process comes down to two components: procedural efficiency and procedural equity. Procedural efficiency is making decisions in an expeditious and direct manner. Little wasted motion is involved. Decision makers home in on key points, come to a decision based on relevant data, and enact the decision without delay and without unnecessary actors involved. Chains of command are direct and easily understood. Support staff and auxiliary entities are minimal. The process is forthright, easily understood, and quick without being hasty.

Procedural equity, on the other hand, involves access, attention, and benefits being allocated in an equitable and just manner. Here the concern is not with decisions being made promptly and without substantial expenditures and support, but with decisions being made with due concern for all who should have influence and not with a special or undue concern for the interests of only some. Put in popular terms, the process must involve listening to ordinary people and not to special interests. Our concept of procedural equity approximates the notion of procedural justice that is popular in some parts of the social-psychology literature. The work of psychologist Tom Tyler is perhaps the best on the topic.

According to Tyler, the central features of procedural justice are "neutrality, lack of bias, honesty, efforts to be fair, politeness, and respect for citizens' rights" (1990: 7). In essence, an important element of process is people's perceptions that decisions have been made fairly, and these perceptions of the fairness of the process are separate from perceptions of the actual substantive decision. Even if the policy outcome goes against a person's interest, his or her assessment of the system will be more positive if the process is perceived as procedurally just.

In a democracy such as that of the United States, the common perception is that the group who "should have" influence is virtually everyone. Thus, procedural equity in such a system requires that people feel that they (and all other people) have the opportunity to be involved in the process should they so desire. Craig (1993: 67) argues, for example, that people evaluate governments in part by the extent "to which they are seen as being open, accessible, and attentive to the views of citizens." People will view the political process as equitable, therefore, if they believe the political system offers them the opportunity to be involved in the process and if they think the process is procedurally just.

Thus, an important component of our "theory" of institutional support is that a powerful determinant of support is the extent to which the process by which decisions are made is perceived to be efficient and equitable in the fashions described above. Support is traceable not just to policy outputs (many of which, we now know, are disappointingly unfamiliar even to voters) but also, and we would say more important, to perceptions of the efficiency and equity of the process itself. Easton is largely unconcerned with the processes of government. For him, the feedback loop comes from system outputs, not from the processes internal to the system. No line in his figures runs from the black box to support, only from outputs to support. Perhaps this is why so little research examines the effects of perceptions of process on system support.

Inattention to components of the political system

This point brings us to our final criticism of existing theory. Easton is adamant in his refusal to analyze support for specific institutions and political structures. Though Easton's terminology has been applied specifically and frequently to legislatures and other political institutions, it would appear Easton does not see it working this way. He almost never mentions specific institutions. Indeed, he has been criticized quite vigorously for his diffidence toward the inner workings of the political system. At several points in his writings Easton reminds readers that "the critical questions for us do not relate to . . . the particular form of the internal structures or processes of the system" (1965a: 115). Inputs, black boxes, and outputs form the core of his analysis. The specific nature of the black box is of only passing concern. (Much later, Easton [1990] attempted to remedy this deficiency, though he still has little to say about specific institutions composing the political system.)

Easton does break down the political system into three potential "objects of support." One of these, the political community, is not relevant to our argument, but the other two clearly are. Easton recognizes that support can be targeted at "the regime" and at what he calls "the authorities" (1965b: 190–219). This insight is useful, and it is unfortunate that subsequent research has become bogged down in the misleading distinction between specific and diffuse support rather than in the potential of different objects of support to habitually generate quite different types of support from people.

One area of research that did not ignore this distinction, however, is the well-known debate between Miller (1974) and Citrin (1974) over the meaning of the decline in trust for government. Did this decline in trust reflect people's rejection of the political system (the regime) or just the rejection of people (leaders) in government at the time? Miller argues that the decline in trust reflected a decline in support of government authorities and the political system itself; Citrin argues that the decline in trust could more accurately be understood as a withdrawal of support from incumbent public officials rather than a decline in system-level support. The controversy to some extent is a product of the limited NES questions on support, but the larger point is that the distinction between the regime and the authorities has been of some use.

Still, the regime/authority dichotomy misses what we believe to be the vital objects of support in modern, developed political systems: political institutions. Institutions are where the regime meets the authorities. They are where individual politicians come together and operate within the strictures each institution has developed. Institutions are neither purely "regime" nor purely "authorities," and each institution is different from the others (for example, they each are perceived by the people to have a different "mix" of regime and authorities). These facts are the source of much confusion when observers attempt to make sense of public attitudes toward institutions. We intend to address very self-consciously the dual identities of political institutions, as well as the unique identities of each institution.

By skipping from regime to authorities as Easton does, or even by focusing on public attitudes toward just one institution as does the research reviewed in the next chapter, a valuable opportunity is missed to elucidate (and learn from) the tremendous variation in support across different types of political institutions. These variations have much to say about how people view politics, about what in politics they like and dislike, and about the health and nature of political systems. As John Wahlke notes, "the level of support for the institutional apparatus of government seems to be another major dimension of regime support" (1971: 271).

AMERICANS' LOVE/HATE RELATIONSHIP WITH DEMOCRACY

When process is viewed as a source of support or lack of support, new vistas emerge. To capitalize on the improved understanding made possible by recognition of the process–support connection, however, it is first necessary to determine the kinds of processes people like and dislike. We have collected a substantial amount of information on this topic, though still not as much as we would like, and we begin to report these findings in Chapter 3. But it is important now to sketch our basic conclusions about the political processes people favor and do not favor. We think these conclusions are surprising.

When previous researchers have attempted to determine people's level of commitment to democratic values, the standard practice has been to focus on freedom of speech (see McClosky, 1964; McClosky & Brill, 1983). This approach is not unreasonable, but a commitment to freedom of speech is hardly commensurate with a commitment to all democratic values, as many more elements of democratic values exist. More important, and as the research on commitment to freedom of speech indicates, a claimed commitment to certain values should not be equated with a commitment at the operational level. We may profess attachment to broad values but react negatively when these values are put into practice in specific instances.

The aspect of democratic values that concerns us most, and that has been largely ignored by previous research, is a commitment to basic democratic processes. We agree with Bernard Crick when he writes that the process of democratic politics involves compromise among competing interests, tolerance of diverse points of view, and "some recognition that government is . . . best conducted amid the open canvassing of rival interests" (1992: 18). This means that democratic processes will not usually highlight certainty, agreement, and speed. Rather, they often reveal our lack of certainty, often remind us of our disagreements, and are seldom speedy.

In addition, the nature of modern democracy in a mass technocratic society is consistent with processes allowing for disagreements, debates, and decisions to be undertaken by *representatives* of various people, causes, and interests rather than by the people themselves. This leaves open the possibility that these representatives will be perceived to have been co-opted, leaving the ordinary people out of the process. Further, though it may not be absolute (and some people, such as the term-limit supporters, are trying to reverse the trend), there is a tendency in developed and differentiated societies for institutions to become complex, bounded, professionalized, and distinguished by unique norms, rules, standard operating procedures, and support structures (see Durkheim, 1947; Polsby, 1968; Weber, 1947).

So, true democratic processes in any realistic environment are bound to be slow, to be built on compromise, and to make apparent the absence of clean, certain answers to important questions of the day. Given the size, nature, and developmental stage of American society, our democratic processes are further characterized by visible agents (representatives of various concerns and people) and less visible principals (the people and concerns themselves), and by elaborate and ponderous governmental structures.

With these core features of democratic processes in mind, we turn to a brief preview of the public's process preferences. To put it simply, Americans tend to dislike virtually all of the democratic processes described above. They dislike compromise and bargaining,[2] they dislike committees and bureaucracy, they dislike political parties and interest groups, they dislike big salaries and big staffs, they dislike slowness and multiple stages, and they dislike debate and publicly hashing things out, referring to such actions as haggling or bickering.

Americans want both procedural efficiency and procedural equity. What seems to escape many people is that democratic processes are practically by definition not procedurally efficient. The "haggling and bickering" so frequently decried by the people could very easily be termed informed discussion. And while eliminating interest groups and political parties might alleviate the sense that equity has been trashed by special interests, it would be impossible for democratic procedures to work in our kind of society without something like them. We need these groups to link the people and the governmental structures unless we want to try direct democracy (and the people do not).

In stressing Americans' distaste for open debate and methodical coalition building as well as their fondness for clear, quick decisions, we are not simply restating the point that most people have authoritarian streaks (see Adorno et al., 1950; Altemeyer, 1988); the situation is more complicated than that. It is not so much that Americans are authoritar-

---

2 Craig also picks up on the public's negative views of compromise, and contrasts these views with those of politicians (1993: 148).

ians in the sense that they crave a "man on a white horse." This would be easy to provide. What Americans want is much more difficult. They want stealth democracy.

They want opportunities for involvement, and they want to know that if they take the opportunity they will be taken seriously. At the same time, they do not really want to get involved. Not only that, they do not really want to have to see the political process being played out. They want democratic decision-making processes in which everyone can voice an opinion, but they do not prefer to see or to hear the debate resulting from the expression of these inevitably diverse opinions. To them, such debate is bickering, haggling, and all talk. They want openness in the sense that they want to know they or anybody else can exercise influence if they want to. They do not want key decisions to be made in private, but this does not mean people are likely to try to influence government or to want to see and hear every laborious step of the governing process. They only want to know that the opportunities exist. The American people want democratic procedures, but they do not want to see them in action.

Do not ever say that people will henceforth be denied the opportunity to observe a congressional committee meeting or that the position of dog catcher or weed commissioner will be turned into a nonelective office. Such proposals are usually opposed vigorously by a loud and substantial majority of Americans. But at the same time, do not infer from this opposition that the public likes to be involved – even in a passive way – in politics. It does not. The people simply do not want to be told that they *cannot* be involved. This desire should not obscure the basic fact that the American public dislikes many of the core features of democratic procedures.

Just as people want governmental services without the pain of taxes, they also want democratic procedures without the pain of witnessing what comes along with those procedures. Political observers have failed to understand this situation no doubt partly because many of us enjoy watching the give and take of politics. In this, we are quite different from ordinary people. They are put off by this same give and take; they do not want it. They want efficient, equitable decisions, and they want them reached in a fashion that does not force them to be exposed to the process. They also want to be confident nobody has been given an inside track or special, undeserved attention. Of course, the belief that politicians are always "haggling and bickering" is fueled by the perception that the process is dominated by special interests. A popular myth is that if members of Congress listened to the people rather than to the special interests, most disagreements would magically disappear. So while it is true that public dissatisfaction may be directed at what is felt to be a perversion of democracy rather than at democratic processes themselves, it is also true that popular assumptions about the cohesiveness of public opinion (and the detachment of special interests from that public opinion) are so unrealistic as to make this point inconsequential. People still wish to avoid the "open canvass" of diverse interests that is unavoidable with democracy.

None of this is to say that the public is displeased with the existing constitutional structure. Quite the contrary. The public still reacts negatively to proposals that would seriously disrupt the institutional relationships outlined in the Constitution even if some of the positions favored by the public seem consistent with a parliamentary structure. But the public draws a distinction between the constitutional outline and the way things are currently working or not working. It believes portions of the original design have been subverted. The problem is not the Constitution; it is that we are not sticking closely enough to the Constitution.

If open debate is seen as bickering and haggling; if bargaining and compromise are seen as selling out on principle; if all support staff and division of labor are needless baggage; if carefully working through problems is sloth; and if all interests somehow become evil special interests, it is easy to see why the public is upset with the workings of the political system.

CONCLUSION

This, then, is a broad-brush summary of our argument. Beginning in Chapter 3 we present evidence supporting our view that people are dissatisfied with the *processes* of government. In that chapter we compare public attitudes toward Congress, the Supreme Court, and the presidency. If what we have said is correct, the institutions with the most visible democratic processes should be the most disliked institutions. We then turn in Chapter 4 to a more focused look at attitudes toward Congress, since it is in many respects the key piece in the puzzle of institutional support.

In Chapters 5, 6, and 7 we shift away from making overall statements about how "the public" feels by recognizing that people vary widely in their attitudes. We explain why they vary the way they do. In Chapter 5 we rely heavily on our focus-group results; in Chapter 6 we utilize traditional sociodemographic variables to explain attitudinal variations and begin to see the crucial role of perceptions of the political process; and in Chapter 7 we modify and employ concepts borrowed from social psychology to pursue the emphasis on process. All this leads to our effort in Chapter 8 to fit the pieces together.

But before any of this, in Chapter 2, we bring the focus down from the general political system to individual institutions, where it will remain for most of this work. As noted previously, we believe much leverage is gained by acknowledging the important role of institutions in the U.S. government and by comparing public attitudes toward these different institutions to learn what the public likes and dislikes. The research and data we review in Chapter 2, while light on interinstitutional comparisons, has attempted to determine the correlates of support for individual institutions but, we argue, has been limited by the availability of suitable longitudinal data.

2

Changing levels of support
for individual institutions

In Chapter 1 we provided an overview of explanations for public dissatisfaction with the entire political system, and a critique of the prevalent theoretical frameworks used to understand that dissatisfaction. In this chapter we offer an overview of research on public attitudes toward individual political institutions, as well as a critique of existing data available to address these attitudes. By the beginning of the third chapter, where we turn to our own data and theorizing, readers should have gained substantial familiarity with the literature and with the theoretical and evidential problems surrounding the important task of understanding the American public's feelings toward its political system and institutions.

THE NEED FOR STUDYING INDIVIDUAL INSTITUTIONS

The more global and impressionistic writings referenced in Chapter 1, while useful, are beset with problems. Some problems flow from the inadequacies of the Eastonian theoretical constructs, and some flow from the fact that the evidence used to support the explanations is simply not up to the challenge. Ehrenhalt, Dionne, and the Kettering Foundation offer only anecdotal support for their views (for a withering critique of the "methodology" employed in the Kettering Report, see Polsby, 1993a); Lipset and Schneider primarily rely upon the narrow and flawed Harris question about confidence in the leaders of institutions; and Miller, Citrin, and Craig all utilize the National Election Studies battery on citizen trust and related concepts – a helpful if somewhat tired set of questions posed only once every two years.

These alleged limitations aside, our approach is quite different from that of most of the research cited to this point. While we are interested in people's feelings toward the overall political arena, our main focus is on public sentiments toward *individual political institutions*, primarily but certainly not exclusively Congress. Why? Although it may sound reductionist, important strides toward understanding perceptions of the whole can be taken by determining attitudes toward the parts. We intend to learn more about public attitudes concerning the overall political system by investigating attitudes toward its components. The U.S. government is built around multiple power bases. We have a presidential, not parliamentary, system, meaning that the executive and legislative branches are elected separately and are distinct institutions. We have an unusually powerful and autonomous court system. And we have a sharing of powers between the central government and a welter of subnational governments.

Forcing people to summarize their evaluations of such a disparate collection of parts in a single judgment is asking far too much. Think of the pressure put on respondents by questions such as, "Would you say that the government is pretty much run by a few big interests looking out for themselves or that it is run for the benefit of all the people?" Suppose the respondent believed that many key members of Congress were susceptible to the influence of "a few big interests" but that the president, the Supreme Court, and certain other members of Congress honestly tried to "benefit all the people." How should the respondent answer? The answer would seem to depend upon a complex calculation of which parts of government are the most powerful as well as how power is distributed within Congress, a tough assignment for even the most reflective observers of the political scene. And this says nothing about varying perceptions across levels of government. How does the respondent answer the question if he or she perceives the federal government to be in the pockets of big interests but views the state government to be serving all?

In light of the distinct institutions composing the U.S. political system, it is essential that we investigate support for each institution. There is no reason to expect each institution to be held in similar public regard (and they are not).[1] Each has a different story. Congress, as we mentioned, is the object of much scorn; we need to know why, both because this information could help us understand attitudes toward the system *and* because Congress is in and of itself an essential actor. A lack of support for an individual institution, just as for the system as a whole, could lead to diminished compliance with outputs, to difficulties in securing members to serve, and to efforts to change structures in crucial

---

1 As Dennis notes, "Images and evaluations of major institutions and structures such as Congress have independent standing in the minds of people in our society" (1981: 321). We leave for another time the varying levels of support for the federal as opposed to state and local governments. For some interesting findings, see Patterson, Ripley, and Quinlan (1992).

regards (for more on these potential consequences, see Craig, 1993: chapter 6; Easton, 1965a,b; Mondak, 1992; Tyler, 1990); but for now it is enough to note that diminished support can lead to dire consequences. In a more general sense, democratic government is built on belief in the value of citizen opinion, so if citizens believe their government, or key parts of it, to be unworthy of support, the situation merits serious investigation.

Given the deserving nature of the topic of public support for political institutions, one might suppose that scholars have addressed it at great length. Here is the real surprise. Although, as will be seen shortly, there has been some scholarly interest in public support for each of the three constitutionally described institutions, there has been almost no interest in building a broader understanding of institutional support. To build such an understanding it is necessary to be consciously comparative – not only to collect information on support for individual institutions but to use that information to make generalizations about the correlates of support.[2] What kinds of institutions tend to be more supported, and under what conditions does institutional support go up or down? The ability to answer such questions is reduced dramatically if the focus is on just one institution, so we have made an effort not only to ascertain public sentiments toward individual institutions (and their parts), we also use this information comparatively to construct a theory of institutional support. In turn, we hope this theory will be a part of general efforts to understand the relationship of citizens to democratic institutions.

The lack of interest in building a theory of institutional support is all the more surprising in light of the current popularity of institutionalism in the study of politics. Many have written of a "new institutionalism" centered around the notion that, unsurprisingly enough, institutions matter. Unfortunately, these scholars have defined much too narrowly the manner in which institutional design and performance can "matter." This definition has been totally fixated on the policy consequences of institutions.

For example, the contributors to R. Kent Weaver and Bert A. Rockman's impressive edited volume entitled *Do Institutions Matter?* (1993) present intrepid views and useful information on the vital question of whether American separation-of-powers systems produce better or worse

2 Wright's critique of Citrin illustrates the bias against analyzing and comparing support for parts of the system. After noting that Citrin distinguishes among current policies, ongoing events, incumbent officeholders, and the entire political system, Wright contends that he finds "these conceptual exercises to be largely beside the point. It is unlikely the mass public entertains any such niceties in their own political thinking" (1976: 73).

policies than parliamentary-type systems. As another example, Mathew McCubbins and Terry Sullivan state that choices about how to structure institutions are "made explicitly to govern the process of policy choice" (1987: 3). Toward what end are these efforts to manipulate policy choice being made? Again quoting McCubbins and Sullivan, "the general theme of . . . most modern studies of institutions is that institutions are designed to enable members to pursue their goals effectively" (1987: 8).

We do not deny that institutional structure can have a substantial influence on the manner in which preferences are aggregated and, therefore, on policy choice. The new institutionalism has introduced a useful vocabulary and a valuable focus into the study of politics. But why has it been unwilling to recognize that institutions matter in ways other than policy? The very nature of institutions and the processes they are seen to embody affect the way citizens feel about their political system. If there is any doubt about this, we intend to dispel it in the rest of this book.

The truth is that institutions can matter quite apart from the policies they produce. A key message of the research we report is that institutions matter because they affect people's perceptions of the political system. Because of the way institutions are shaped, because of the images they project, and because of the processes they are perceived to employ, the public reacts either more or less favorably to them. These reactions to individual institutions and their component parts, in turn, are related to public opinion of the political system as a whole. In fact, it just may be that public reaction to the structure and processes of the system is more vital (and direct) than the frequently minor policy effects possibly traceable to institutional choice (see Rogowski, 1987; Weaver & Rockman, 1993).

But new institutionalists are not the only ones to ignore the importance of institutional structure and process on public attitudes. Even research on public mood focuses heavily on policy and often ignores public attitudes toward institutions. For example, James Stimson's (1991) influential book, *Public Opinion in America,* has as its main goal the explication of "the public mood." But for Stimson this mood is defined in terms of Left/Right policy positions. In collecting data to discern the public mood, Stimson excludes all questions not dealing with "issue preferences" (1991: 35). His vision of public opinion is that it "is about as institution-free as anything in politics can be" (1991: xix). This general approach is also found in Benjamin Page and Robert Shapiro's recent work, as is apparent in the title: *The Rational Public: Fifty Years of Trends in Americans' Policy Preferences* (1992). No research on the public's institutional preferences and reactions exists, let alone any with gravity parallel to the policy work of Stimson, and of Page and Shapiro.

Can anyone deny that an important part of "the public mood" in the 1990s is an intense dissatisfaction with the U.S. political system? This dissatisfaction is not necessarily related to liberal or to conservative attitudes (in fact, we will demonstrate that the connection is fairly weak); moreover, we believe the dissatisfaction with existing political institutions to be far more visceral and consequential than location on an amorphous and increasingly anachronistic ideological spectrum. For much of the populace, terms like liberal and conservative are not overly meaningful. This absence of meaning was suggested in Converse's work of several decades ago (1964) but is even more apropos today, with the end of the Cold War and with what seems to be a de facto consensus on the rough percentage of the U.S. economy that should be accounted for by governmental spending.

The most prevalent area of study in public opinion, however, is vote choice. The literature addressing the question of why people vote the way they do is immense and of high quality, perhaps partly because the resources devoted to this question have been extensive. From National Science Foundation grants to questions asked by the Survey Research Center, among other polling organizations; from articles in the major academic journals to *The American Voter* (Campbell, Converse, Miller, & Stokes, 1960), the core of the study of American politics has been research on the act of voting for individual politicians. How do people perceive candidates? Which candidates do they like, and why? Which candidates do they vote for, and why?

If it is important to know what the public likes and dislikes about particular officeholders (and we think it is), why is it not important to know how the public views the institutions these politicians inhabit or hope to inhabit? Most studies of voting behavior focus solely on voters or "likely voters," thereby excluding half of the adult population, but we believe the perceptions of voters *and* nonvoters alike are extremely important. Nonvoters as well as voters harbor attitudes toward political institutions, and these attitudes matter even if they are not channeled through the traditional act of voting. By visiting with fellow workers, by making comments to their families, by answering questions, by calling or listening to radio talk-show programs, and by generally being a part of society, nonvoters contribute to the political ambience of the country – and this says nothing about the many people who do not vote but are still participating in the political process in other ways (contacting officials or working in local or national efforts of some kind, to mention just two possibilities). Providing support for or opposition to political institutions is something we all do, albeit for some the support or opposition is so minimal as to give the impression that they are inert.

This neglected area of public-opinion research is even more important given that political institutions are at the center of the American polity. In fact, we are occasionally told that the American political system has, for better or for worse, been subjected to the process of institutionalization (see, for example, Huntington, 1965 and Polsby, 1968, on the Congress; Schmidhauser, 1973, on the Supreme Court; King & Ragsdale, 1988, on the institutionalized presidency; and Eisenstadt, 1964, for a more general treatment). Without going into too much detail, this process involves institutions becoming more established, permanent, elaborate, and autonomous. Given the persuasive evidence marshaled by these scholars in support of the institutionalization thesis, it is all the more surprising that public perceptions of these more clearly defined and autonomous institutions have not come in for a corresponding amount of attention.

Strongly adverse public sentiments toward certain institutions could conceivably inspire efforts to reform those institutions in fundamental ways. For example, direct elections were successfully thrust upon a reluctant Senate because people widely perceived it to be dominated by trusts and men of privilege. Roosevelt's court-packing scheme caused changes in the voting behavior of Justices Hughes and Roberts partly because low public esteem for the court at that time made it vulnerable. And the more recent movement to limit the terms of state and national legislators is connected to the perception that legislatures are not working properly. Further, other institutions may become emboldened at the sight of a struggling fellow institution, thereby leading to altered institutional relationships.

And coming to grips with public perceptions of institutions is important not just because of the implications these perceptions have for the structure and operations of the institutions themselves. Rather, public attitudes toward the major political institutions affect public attitudes toward the entire political system as well as toward individual politicians. It is only natural that a person would tend to be less favorably disposed toward the overall political system if that person perceived one or more of the institutions composing that system to be deeply flawed.

As to institutional perceptions coloring the activities of individual politicians (for evidence that such a relationship exists, at least in Congress, see Born, 1990), potential candidates may decline to seek an office that is not held in high regard. Those already in such an office may choose to retire voluntarily, or they may be more reluctant to assume unpopular stances due to understandable concerns with their own status and that of the institution. In other words, it is not difficult to imagine low levels of support for political institutions leading to a lower quality of public servant as well as to a lessened institutional capacity to withstand demands from the public and from other, less-disliked quarters of the political system. Such logic undergirds much of the research on political support. In light of these potentially serious ramifications, we are led, once again, to register our puzzlement over the lack of systematic scholarship on public perceptions of political institutions.

By ignoring attitudes toward institutions and the political system, and by not considering that institutions matter because they affect the public's perceptions of the system and the institutions themselves, we are not only missing a major element of the current polity, we are decreasing our chances of formulating an appropriate theoretical framework for understanding the nexus between the public and democratic governmental apparatuses. Because these apparatuses, by common consent, have become more elaborate and separate from the people, this nexus promises to be an increasingly weak link in the democratic chain and, as a result, demands our full attention.

In the next chapter we begin in earnest to present our modest contribution to what we see as an extremely important task. In the remainder of this chapter, however, we describe research and data that have previously been generated on public support for individual institutions. The research on individual institutions is distinct from more general efforts (summarized in Chapter 1) to describe public unrest with the whole political enterprise. Miller (1974) and Citrin (1974), for example, may disagree on whether the public simply distrusts the people in government at a particular time (Citrin) or is also turning away from the political institutions themselves (Miller); but they both adopt an undifferentiated view of institutions. Never do these analysts seriously entertain the possibility that support for certain institutions may be substantially lower than support for others, or that certain people may be more likely to support certain kinds of institutions. This undifferentiated view of very differentiated political institutions is quite similar to Easton's view.

But there does exist a respectably sized pocket of research that peers beneath the too-broad concept of political system to look at individual institutions. Our only criticism of this research is that it has not been eager enough to view public support for political institutions in something other than a seriatim fashion. Still, the good news is that this research shares our belief that there comes a point when we must roll up our sleeves, recognize that in the United States both the separation of powers and the federal structure provide numerous, distinct elements of "government," and try to sort through people's attitudes toward these distinct institutions. And the three federal institutions *are* distinct. They occupy very different portions of the polity, and possess structures and standard operating procedures that could hardly be more different. Not surprisingly, distinct research approaches and problems are associated with each institution.

PREVIOUS RESEARCH ON SUPPORT FOR
INDIVIDUAL INSTITUTIONS

Existing research on attitudes toward individual political institutions in the United States could perhaps be characterized as spotty, but it provides a start on the path toward a theory of public support for political institutions. The usual approach is to determine the overall level of support for an institution in a certain year by turning to survey results. Comparable figures for other years are then recorded and variations in the level of support are explained in traditional time-series fashion, with a varied assortment of independent variables. The key question such designs are meant to answer is why support for an institution is higher in some years than in others.

But institutional differences (and data availability) produce distinct stories for each institution. In the case of the executive branch, almost nothing exists on public support for the institution itself. Much attention has been devoted to support for the person occupying the position of president, but not so for the institution of the presidency. The Harris polling organization cannot even decide how to word its question about confidence in the presidency. Sometimes it asks about confidence in the White House; other times it asks about confidence in the executive branch; and still other times it asks both questions. What do people envision when asked these questions? The entire bureaucracy? Political appointees? The cabinet? The president only? Ordinary citizens almost certainly think of the president when they are passing judgment on something called the White House or on the executive branch. To obtain views on the presidency as distinct from the current president, more carefully focused questions would need to be asked.

Absent such questions, scholars have done the sensible thing and concentrated on explaining different levels of support for the sitting president. An impressive literature has grown up around the topic of presidential popularity. We know that, while there is wide variation from president to president, most enjoy high public support early in their terms, before support dwindles with the passage of the months. Temporary adjustments in this pattern can be produced by decisive presidential actions, by economic conditions, by wars, and by other relevant conditions and actions (see, for example, Bond, Fleisher, & Northrup, 1988; Kernell, 1978; MacKuen, 1983; Mueller, 1973; Ostrom & Simon, 1985). And the pattern for some presidents – notably Eisenhower and Reagan – has not followed the usual twists and turns.

Existing research on support for the Supreme Court looks quite different, as well it should. Perceptions of the Court are not so much centered on one person; in fact, they are not so much centered on people at all. Citizens are not particularly familiar with the personnel of the Court. But support for the Court in general is of considerable interest given the difficult position in which it has been placed by the drafters of the Constitution. Lacking the legitimacy of elections and given its responsibility to act without substantial regard for public opinion, the Court is in some ways vulnerable. As a result, there has been sustained interest in the ability of the Court to generate support.

Much of this research has been conceptual, although a few studies have drawn on actual soundings of public attitudes. One of the more concerted efforts to determine the predictors of aggregate levels of support for the Supreme Court was conducted by Gregory Caldeira (1986; see also Davis, 1994: chapter 1; Dolbeare & Hammond, 1968; Handberg, 1984; Kessel, 1966; Murphy & Tanenhaus, 1968; Tanenhaus & Murphy, 1981, for a sampling of the better work). Caldeira concludes that while people, due to lack of knowledge and attention, "base judgments on the vaguest and crudest of ideological frameworks," the public "appears to respond to events on the political landscape and to actions taken by the Supreme Court" (1986: 1223).

Less work has been done on public support for the U.S. Congress. In fact, as will be discussed in the next chapter, strange as it may seem, we may know more about the intricacies and correlates of public support for the Iowa state legislature than we do for the U.S. Congress. Early work by Davidson, Kovenock, and O'Leary (1968), Davidson and Parker (1972), and Parker (1977), and later work by Patterson and Caldeira (1990), Bowman and Ladd (1992), and Asher and Barr (1993), all point generally to the same conclusion (see also Patterson & Magleby, 1992). Support for Congress varies from year to year and seems to be at least partially a function of public attitudes toward the president, to scandals, to the economy, and to perceived presidential-congressional relations (see especially Patterson & Caldeira, 1990: 42; but also Davidson, Kovenock, & O'Leary, 1968: 52; Durr, Gilmour, & Wolbrecht, 1994).

Taken together, the main conclusions from previous research attempting to explain variation in aggregate support for political institutions are that support depends to some extent on the actions and policy decisions of those in the institutions, on the nature of the times (the condition of the economy, for example), and perhaps on the level of support for other institutions (see Baas, 1980; Davidson, Kovenock, & O'Leary, 1968: 59–63). But the precise actions, policy decisions, and conditions found relevant to support vary widely from study to study perhaps partly because specifications and variables are not consistent across the studies. And none of this is particularly relevant to the larger picture since these studies focus specifically on one institution or another. No effort is made to compare support for the various institutions, to determine if some institutions are more responsive than others to particular independent variables, or even to speculate on what we should expect to find if such comparisons were undertaken. In short, if part of the enterprise is to develop a theory of public support for institutions,[3] analyzing the institutions individually will not do the trick.

The major exception to this approach is Lipset and Schneider's important work, *The Confidence Gap* (1987).[4] Though most of that book is concerned with nonpolitical institutions such as medicine, education, the military, organized religion, major companies, the press, and organized labor, portions of it do address political institutions. The data they present, most of it from Harris, make a strong case that confidence in leaders of all kinds of institutions move roughly together and that the direction in which they moved together over the past thirty years was generally down (except in the mid-1980s, when there was a temporary rebound). They even make a brief pass at determining varying levels of sensitivity to salient economic conditions like unemployment and inflation. For example, they conclude that support for Congress and the executive branch are slightly more connected to these economic conditions than support for the Supreme Court, just as most observers would predict.

CHANGES OVER TIME IN SUPPORT FOR CONGRESS, THE COURT, AND THE PRESIDENT

Rather than relying on interpretations provided in previous research, matters can be clarified by the graphic presentation of relevant data. Figure 2.1 shows that the public traditionally has substantially more confidence in the Supreme Court than it does in Congress. In fact, since Harris began (in the 1960s) more or less regularly asking questions about confidence in the leaders of various institutions, the Supreme Court has always been accorded more confidence than Congress. The mean percentage with a great deal of confidence in the Supreme Court is 30, and the range is from 22 to 50. The mean percentage with a great deal of confidence in Congress is just 17, and the range is from 8 to 42.

The extra confidence placed in the Supreme Court is consistent and actually quite sizable in light of the truncated variance accompanying the fairly low levels of confidence in everything. The Gallup organization

3 To be fair to the studies mentioned, this was not their purpose.
4 Other exceptions include Caldeira and Gibson, 1992; Davidson, Kovenock, and O'Leary, 1968; Dennis, 1973, 1981; and Patterson, Ripley, and Quinlan, 1992. Some of these will be addressed in the next chapter.

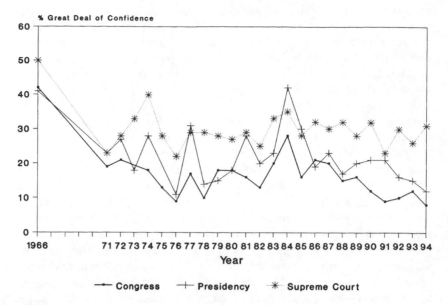

Figure 2.1. Confidence in Congress, the presidency, and the Supreme Court

question, asked less frequently but not stressing the leaders of the institutions, reveals an identical pattern. The public has more confidence in the Supreme Court than in Congress; on this there can be little doubt.

What about the executive branch? Like the Supreme Court, more confidence is usually placed in the executive branch than in the Congress; the mean percentage with a great deal of confidence in the executive branch is 22, and the range is 11 to 42. But, as might be expected, confidence in the executive branch is by far the most volatile and "personality-dependent."[5] Given the hierarchical structure of the presidency, confidence in the person occupying the pinnacle of that institution will obviously go a long way toward determining confidence in the entire executive branch. As a result, while confidence in the executive branch is usually greater than confidence in the Congress and less than confidence in the Supreme Court, it is more volatile; it bounced above confidence in the Court on two occasions (1977 and 1984), and sunk below confidence in the Congress on two occasions (1979 and 1986). Still, the general pattern is clearly for the public to be least confident in Congress

5 The Harris question refers specifically to confidence in the leadership of the "White House," except in a small number of years when the question refers instead to the "executive branch of the federal government." Based on the few years in which both wordings were used it would appear that the language does not produce wildly different results.

and most confident in the Supreme Court; confidence in the executive careens somewhere between these two.

Another noteworthy aspect of these patterns is the virtual absence of any upward or downward trend since the mid-1970s. If a regression line is fit to the time-series for each institution from 1975 to 1994 (20 data points), the unstandardized slope for confidence in the Supreme Court is actually mildly positive (.11); but the more important findings are that it would take more than nine years to produce a 1-percent increase in confidence and that the coefficient is not close to being significant ($t = .89$).

The story is not much different for the other institutions. Confidence in the executive branch produces a mildly negative slope when regressed on time (1975–94), but the coefficient is small ($-.21$) and not significant ($t = -.64$). The insignificant slope and nonexistent explanatory power of time is also apparent when the dependent variable is confidence in the Congress. The slope again is slightly negative ($-.17$) and insignificant ($t = -.87$).

The clear message is that in the twenty years between 1975 and 1994, confidence in the three major institutions of the federal government moved neither up nor down. The biggest exception to this statement was an increase in confidence appearing around 1984 and apparently led by confidence in Ronald Reagan and the executive branch; but for the most part these decades produced no major changes in confidence levels. As a result, from 1975 on, the mean percentages of those having great confidence in the Supreme Court, the presidency, and Congress (29 percent, 21 percent, and 15 percent, respectively) are generally reflective of public opinion over the entire twenty-year period.

But this apparent stability only highlights the steep drop in confidence in all three institutions occurring between 1966 and 1971. In February of 1966, 42 percent of all respondents claimed to have "a great deal of confidence" in the people running Congress. The story was virtually the same in January of 1967, when 41 percent (of "voters only" in this particular survey) claimed to have a great deal of confidence. Contrast this with the situation four years later, when only 19 percent of all respondents had a great deal of confidence in the people running Congress.

Because stability has settled in since the mid-1970s, it goes without saying that confidence has never recovered from this drop. Only twice since 1971 have more than 25 percent claimed a great deal of confidence in Congress – in September of 1973, when the nation was enmeshed in the Watergate scandal, and in November of 1984, as Reagan feel-goodism and a strong economy apparently affected popular perceptions of the leaders of Congress. More often than not, confidence drifts in the low teens and occasionally even below. It is clear that all the other changes in recent attitudes are dwarfed by the drop in confidence between 1967 and 1971.

It is also obvious that Lipset and Schneider (1987) are generally correct in calling attention to the breadth of the decline at this time in support for all institutions – or virtually all. Congress may have dropped 23 points in these four years, but the Supreme Court dropped 17 and the executive branch dropped 14, with more to come two years later, after Watergate. Confidence in the leaders of nonpolitical institutions did not fare much better. Leaders of the educational community dropped 19 points, major companies dropped 20, organized religion 13, and leaders of the military dropped the most – 29 points. The mean drop was 14 points, so although Congress dropped more than the mean, it is important to place the change in context. This was a time of declining confidence in the leaders of most American institutions.

But just what was it about the 1967–71 period? Obviously, it was not Watergate, for the burglary transpired in 1972 and did not become widely known until the summer of 1973. Was it the tumultuous Democratic convention and contentious three-way general election contest of 1968, the race riots, the assassinations, the Vietnam War? If Harris's "confidence in institutional leaders" question had been asked with greater frequency, or if Gallup had begun asking its confidence-in-institutions question prior to 1973, we would be much better positioned to answer these questions and, therefore, to understand more about when and why attitudes toward institutions changed.

But this is not the case. Instead, data are the sparsest right where we need them to be the most dense. As a result, we must turn to less central questions in the hope that some sense of the precise timing and causes of the change between 1967 and 1971 can be patched together. In every year since 1963, excepting 1972, Harris has asked the public to evaluate the job performance of Congress. Was it excellent, pretty good, only fair, or poor? Job performance is obviously not the same as confidence in an institution or in the leaders of an institution, but it is not unrelated. When we have information on both confidence and job performance, they appear to move in rough tandem (see also Patterson & Caldeira, 1990).

Job performance provides a valuable clue to the notorious drop in confidence in the leaders of Congress – and perhaps the leaders of other institutions. It suggests that the 1965–67 period may have been unusual in its high level of support for Congress, and that the drop in support after 1967 was mostly a return to more normal levels. The public's evaluation of congressional job performance in 1963 and 1964 was quite low before rising sharply in 1965, 1966, and, to a lesser extent, 1967.

34

For whatever reasons, perhaps because of Congress's high level of legislative activity, it would appear that 1965 and 1966 were years in which
the public rated congressional job performance more highly than it ever
has (at least since the beginning of systematic polling).

Additional support for our reading of the situation is provided by a
look at even earlier opinion data, although relevant data were collected
only in scattered years before 1963. For example, we know that in 1953
(perhaps because of the cessation of the Korean conflict) Congress's job
approval was high, but that by 1954 it was very low again. Even during
World War II public approval of Congress was faint – and after the war
approval sank to levels almost, but not quite, as low as in the 1970s
and 1980s. The small number and erratic spacing of the data prior to
1971 make conclusions difficult, but it does seem that there are only a
few brief periods of strong approval of the job being done by Congress,
and one of these periods is indeed the mid-1960s.

So the low levels of positive feelings for Congress in the past twenty
years may be slightly more extreme and persistent than usual, but the
historical norm – to the extent it can be determined from these irregular
data – is for quite modest levels of support. Moreover, when support is
reasonably high it is only for fleeting periods, perhaps a year or two (on
this point, see also Davidson, Kovenock, & O'Leary, 1968: chapter 2).
These job-performance figures at least raise the possibility that the drop
in confidence from 1967 to 1971 might look large not because confidence in 1971 was abnormally low but because confidence in 1966–67
was abnormally high. Of course, this does not negate the fact that confidence is still quite low, but it does put a different light on how historically novel this low level might be. We suspect that the 1965–67 period
was in actuality the atypical time as concerns support for Congress.

The first part of 1995 is another example of an atypical time. Though
we write this before release of the 1995 Harris "confidence" numbers,
similar survey questions, such as the *Washington Post*/ABC News job-
approval question asked at the end of January (Morin, 1995), indicated
an increase in public support for Congress to levels higher than they had
been for more than three years. Harris is quite likely to report an increase
in public confidence in Congress given that the question will be posed
just a few weeks after the much-ballyhooed coronation of a brand new
majority party and leadership team. But all indications are that this increase will be ephemeral. Indeed, the *Washington Post*/ABC News poll
mentioned above detected that this "cooling" process was already un-
derway by the end of January, 1995. A return to more traditional low-
confidence survey responses is a certainty.

The story is much the same for the other two branches of government.
Figure 2.1 indicates that confidence in the leaders of the Supreme Court

dropped sharply between 1967 and 1971, increased after Watergate, dropped a little, and then increased in the mid-1980s, thus nearly duplicating the general pattern found with congressional support. Meanwhile, confidence in the leaders of the executive branch also dropped in the early 1970s and on through the Watergate events, and stayed fairly low after that, with noticeable blips up around the beginning of each new presidential term and in 1984.

Comparing trends across institutions underscores the belief that their fortunes are connected. The spikes in 1967 and 1984 are present for all three institutions, and the absence of much movement in many other years is more than coincidental, right down to the gradual drop in support since 1984. Davidson, Kovenock, and O'Leary would seem to be on the right track when they state that "public approval is usually highest when domestic political controversy is muted. . . . When partisan controversy is especially acrimonious, or when Congress seems slow in resolving legislation, public disaffection increases" (1968: 52–53).

But these similarities and connections should not be taken as implying that we can treat all institutions the same in terms of public support. Overall levels tend to be quite different across institutions. The degree of volatility is also quite different, and there are instances in which institutional support moves in opposite directions. In 1973, for example, confidence in the White House dropped while confidence in Congress and the Supreme Court shot up. Then, in 1974, support for Congress dipped while support for the White House and the Supreme Court increased markedly. Even if the patterns were identical, the "normal" levels of support for the three institutions are quite different. So, by looking at aggregated data we learn that the three institutions each have unique levels and, to a lesser extent, patterns of support. But the problems with these aggregated data must not be ignored.

PROBLEMS WITH EXISTING DATA

Existing time-series data face several major problems. First, the wording of survey questions has been inconsistent and erratic across studies. We see three potential problems here: the referent of the question, the available response options, and the evaluative term used. The referents asked about by Harris, Gallup, and others have differed. The Harris questions, which have been used most frequently in the longitudinal studies we have been describing, stress confidence in the *leaders* of institutions. Gallup, on the other hand, draws attention to the institutions themselves: "I am going to read you a list of institutions in American society. Would you tell me how much respect and confidence you, yourself, have in each one – a great deal, quite a lot, some, or very little?" Changing the referent from leaders to the institution and changing the number of response options from three to four theoretically could severely alter the responses generated.

As it turns out, changing the referents may not matter much, whereas changing the number of response options might. Lipset and Schneider (1987: 89–93) report the results of an experiment designed to determine the impact of both the specific referent and the number of options. Administering altered versions of the question to a split sample, they reach the initially surprising conclusion that, while the institution as referent is usually seen a little more favorably than the people or leaders of that institution, the differences are extremely small. They conclude that the most significant artifactual shift comes by virtue of moving from three to four options. We believe we can explain why a focus on the leaders, as opposed to a focus on the institution generically, could produce such similar results, and we have more to say about this in Chapter 3. For now, we can say there has been little consistency across surveys, and that available response options may have significant effects on responses.

A potential problem that has not been studied systematically is the impact of various evaluative terms on people's responses. Some surveys have used "confidence," whereas others have used "trust," "respect," or "support." It is difficult to know if these terms are or are not interchangeable. Can someone trust an institution but not respect it? Probably. But we have no evidence on whether the use of one evaluative term or another changes the results much – and previous research seldom says anything about the selection and interpretation of these various terms.

Even if these questions are not flawed, they are extremely limited in their ability to evince nuanced public attitudes on public support for parts of the political system. It would be as if the vote-choice literature had been built on a battery of questions asking about respect/confidence/trust/support for shabbily defined bunches of candidates for different offices – with no questions on the perceived strengths, weaknesses, and visibility of these candidates. Then, this battery would have been posed just once a year for only the past couple of decades, leading researchers to treat each sounding (usually derived over just a two-week period) as though it represented the whole year and could be "accounted for" with explanatory variables derived from far distant portions of that year.[6]

6 The problems with this practice are revealed by one of the few instances in which the question was asked more than once a year. In 1989, Harris asked their "confidence in the leaders of the Supreme Court" question a second time. The motivation was interest in the repercussions of the Court's controversial decisions on abortion (Webster) and flag burning, both announced during the summer of 1989. Before the decisions were announced in early June of 1989, 28 percent of respondents professed a great deal of confidence in the Supreme Court, whereas this figure

Further imagine that this battery was first asked in what we now know to be an atypical year, and we would have to conclude the vote choice research was in trouble. Happily, this is not true of research on voting behavior; unhappily, it is true of research on public support for political institutions.

The bottom line is that nearly all the studies described (as well as Figure 2.1) are based on data not adequate for the careful analyses of variations in support, with the exception of support for sitting presidents. Conclusions about public support for the institutions themselves are based on less-than-perfect questions asked irregularly beginning in an atypical year (1966). Existing time-series data may therefore create an inaccurate vision of a startling decline in support that would, with appropriate data, quite likely appear to be a much less notable decline from an unusually supportive period.

CONCLUSION

Existing analyses of these data have gone as far as they can and perhaps farther than they should have, given deficiencies in the data base. Moreover, while it is natural to be curious about why confidence is higher in some years than in others, this is really not among the most crucial questions surrounding the nature of public support for political institutions. Even if we had answers to this question, this line of research would still tell us nothing about the kind of individual most likely to grant or to deny support, the parts of institutions people tend to like and dislike, or the potential for increasing support by enacting reforms.

The longitudinal approach to studying support is further limited by the muted variation in support since 1971. In the quarter-century since then, support for Congress has always been between 8 and 28 percent; support for the Court between 22 and 40 percent; and support for the presidency between 11 and 42 percent (11 and 31 percent if we exclude

dropped to just 15 percent in mid-July after the two controversial decisions. If reliance were based solely upon the normal yearly soundings, we would have missed an important demonstration that support for the Court can be influenced in a fairly dramatic fashion by its actions. By June of 1990, the next "regular" survey on the topic, much of the negative reaction may have dissipated. Indeed, this would seem to be the case, because confidence in the Supreme Court was back up to 32 in 1990. While timing is crucial with cross-sectional data (such as ours) as well as with the time-series data just critiqued, the particular problem of doing time-series on a widely spaced dependent variable arises from the fact that a yearly data point is often passed off as being representative of that whole year even though, as we have just seen, reactions may differ at various times of the year when many of the explanatory variables are measured at different times of the year when support may have fluctuated. Cross-sectional survey data studies generally draw their dependent and independent variables at the same time.

1984). These numbers suggest that support is far from static but also that it is largely locked into a reasonably constrained low level for all institutions, particularly Congress. If we begin in 1971, when soundings began to be taken more regularly, there is little to talk about save some mildly unusual variations during Watergate and the Reagan blip of 1984. These two anomalies aside, the primary pattern since 1971 is one of desultory and slightly downward movement in support.

None of this is to say that adequate longitudinal data would not be desirable. They most definitely would be. But two points are essential. First, adequate data are not available. Second, even if we had decent time-series data, we would not be in a position to dissect motivations for institutional support in the fashion needed. The tool is too blunt – and the shift over time is not the main concern. In light of the inadequate longitudinal data and of the need to go beyond aggregate figures in order to dig more deeply into the attitudes, perceptions, and desires of the people, we have turned to cross-sectional data of both an intensive and extensive nature, and this is what we report in the rest of this book. The main disadvantage of this approach is that at the end of our work it is likely readers still will not know why support has changed as it has over the years.

But this disadvantage is more than outweighed by the advantages. Attitudes toward political institutions are not something ordinary Americans wear on their sleeves, and they certainly are not captured with a terse question or two about confidence in leaders or about perceptions of job performance. A battery of carefully designed questions is in order, and even then, this survey information should be supplemented with efforts to listen to the people. If we have learned nothing else from survey research it is that we must be very careful to avoid asking respondents to provide more than they are capable of providing because they will fail to admit that they are not up to the question. Extended sessions with ordinary citizens will allow us to learn more about what they do and do not know and about what real attitudes happen to lie behind snap responses to key words.

When attitudes are not easily forthcoming, care must be taken to make sure that what *is* forthcoming is something real. The nature of our particular topic requires extra care in this regard. We can learn only so much from the fact that most people say they do not have confidence in the leaders of our government. We can learn only so much from slight variations over time in the precise percentage with and without confidence. A true and accurate portrait of public attitudes toward political institutions and the system requires in-depth survey questions and in-depth conversations with ordinary people.

Only then will we have a chance of understanding how the people really feel, what it would take to make them feel different, and why some people have different attitudes and perceptions than others. With this information in tow, we may begin to see the big picture of the relationship between the American people and their government, for this relationship is not revealed in studies of voting behavior or congruence between policy attitudes and congressional roll-call behavior. Rather, a major part of this relationship is people's attitudes toward the structures and processes of the political system. This topic is dominating the political scene for ordinary people, but it is hardly being noticed in scholarly research. We now turn to our attempts to contribute to the big picture of public perceptions of and attitudes toward the three major political institutions of the federal government.

3

Perceptions of political institutions

If we know the American public to be fed up, disgusted, and repulsed by Congress and the political system, why should we waste our time explaining public evaluations of political institutions? We already know the whole story, right? Wrong. We actually know very little. Unquestionably, as of the mid-1990s there were plenty of negative feelings toward Congress and government, but saying, for example, that the public "hates" its government is not particularly informative. Hate is an imprecise word, and the U.S. government is an extremely complex entity. Feelings toward some institutions of the government may be quite different from feelings toward others, just as feelings toward aspects of an individual institution may be quite different from feelings toward other aspects of it. Our two major goals in this chapter are to provide a better description of public attitudes than is conveyed in popular accounts and to use this information to begin to sort through what Americans like and dislike in their institutions and why.

But this task is not easily accomplished. For the most part, scholars have lacked the theory and the data necessary to provide a rich portrait of public attitudes toward diverse political institutions. One notable exception is Samuel C. Patterson, Ronald D. Hedlund, and G. Robert Boynton's concerted effort to provide a complete picture of public perceptions of the Iowa state legislature (1975). They conducted an original survey of 1,000 Iowans during the fall of 1966 in which the interviewers posed a fairly detailed set of questions on support for the Iowa legislature. This survey was actually part of a larger data-collection effort in which the legislators themselves were interviewed along with several groups of "elites." Accordingly, much of the authors' attention is devoted to comparing the various attitudes of these different sets of elites and the public. Still, the questions posed by Patterson, Hedlund, and Boynton, even though they were asked more than a quarter of a century ago in only one state, may be the most detailed questions ever asked about public support for a political institution.

With this exception in mind, it is important to note that numerous media and popular polling organizations have described recent public dissatisfaction by utilizing a variety of survey questions that, unfortunately, are seldom analyzed in the requisite multivariate fashion, sometimes for want of appropriate explanatory variables in the brief questionnaires. In addition, recent scholarly research has just begun to adopt a more cross-sectional and cross-institutional approach, as is evident in Patterson, Ripley, and Quinlan's comparison of support for the Congress and for the Ohio state legislature (1992), and Caldeira and Gibson's brief reference to support for the Supreme Court compared to other societal institutions (1992: 647).[1] We share with this recent research the belief that further answers to questions regarding the nature and causes of public support for different institutions will have to come from cross-sectional data with more probing questions. As a result, we have collected a substantial amount of original data to provide us with the information we need. In the summer and fall of 1992, we gathered two original data sets: a nationwide telephone survey of 1,400 adults that lasted approximately thirty minutes; and eight focus-group sessions in four different parts of the United States, each consisting of eight to ten people and lasting about two hours (see the Appendix for a description of these data sets). These data allow us to dig more deeply than ever before into public attitudes toward federal political institutions.

BE CAREFUL WHAT YOU ASK: SPECIFYING REFERENTS

We ascertained people's evaluations of Congress both with a simple approval question and with a feeling thermometer. Approval seems more neutral than terms such as trust, confidence, or respect, which have been used almost interchangeably in previous research. And the feeling thermometer gives people 100 options with which to approximate their true sentiments. More important, recognizing the dual nature of organizations such as Congress, the Supreme Court, and the presidency, we included separate questions on the members of the bodies and then on the

---

1 This cross-sectional work by Patterson, Ripley, and Quinlan (1992) and by Caldeira and Gibson (1992) is less confident about the impact of specific conditions and policy decisions on support than was found in the longitudinal work (sometimes by the same authors). Caldeira and Gibson conclude, for example, that "the mass public does not seem to condition its basic loyalty toward the Court as an institution upon the satisfaction of demands for particular policies or ideological positions. . . . The mass public does not evince this oft-reported connection" (1992: 659). For earlier cross-section, cross-institutional references, see Davidson, Kovenock, and O'Leary (1968: 50) and Dennis (1973).

institutions themselves. This last point deserves additional comment, particularly in light of conventional wisdom.

Richard F. Fenno, Jr. (1975) calls attention to an important situation that is now part of most discussions of public opinion toward Congress: namely, that many Americans claim to harbor negative views of Congress at the same time they profess positive views of their own member of Congress. Why so many citizens adopt this unusual juxtaposition of views came to be known as Fenno's paradox. One of Fenno's answers is that "we apply different standards of judgment, those that we apply to the individual being less demanding than those we apply to the institution" (1975: 278; see also Cook, 1979; Parker & Davidson, 1979; Ripley et al., 1992). Fenno's point is an important one and has quite rightly been influential. Our data confirm, as if confirmation were needed, the basic thrust of the "own member/whole institution" distinction.

Still, we wish to suggest that Fenno's point captures only a part of the overall story. Contrary to first appearances, the distinction people commonly make is not really between their member of Congress and Congress itself; rather, it is between their member and all members – and there is no doubt that people are much more fond of their member than of members generically. To explain this situation properly, it is necessary to ask people to respond to questions containing very specific referents.

Therefore, we asked people about their approval of (and the warmth of feelings toward) members of Congress generally. We then repeated the question with regard to the members of the Supreme Court and George Bush. The specific approval question was: "Thinking about people in government, please tell me if you strongly approve, approve, disapprove, or strongly disapprove of the way the people are handling their jobs."

Similarly, the first feeling-thermometer question made clear reference to the people in the institutions. "I'd like to get your feelings toward some groups of people in the U.S. government. I'll read the name of a group and I'd like you to rate it using something we call the feeling thermometer. Ratings between 50 and 100 degrees mean that you feel favorable and warm toward that group. Ratings between 0 and 50 degrees mean that you don't feel favorable toward the group and that you don't care too much for that group." The language for both the approval and the feeling-thermometer questions is quite common. The novel feature is that we very clearly specified the referent we wanted respondents to evaluate. In other words, the referent was not something amorphous like "Congress," but was the people in Congress.

Then, in separate questions, we ascertained respondents' approval of and warmth of feeling toward the *institutions* of government, not the people in them. This distinction comes fairly naturally to most political scientists, but is not often made by ordinary citizens. We assume that, in general, most people are not accustomed to thinking about institutions of government as something separate from the people composing them. As a result, our survey questions on institutions qua institutions needed to be prefaced, but obviously this introduction needed to be made in a way that was not leading – a difficult assignment.

The language we settled on was as follows: "Now, I've asked you to rate some people in government, but sometimes when we talk about parts of the government in Washington, like the Supreme Court, the presidency, and the Congress, we don't mean the people currently serving in office, we mean the institutions themselves, no matter who's in office. These institutions have their own buildings, historical traditions, and purposes laid out in the Constitution. I'd like to know how warm or cold you feel toward these institutions, not the people currently in office." No language could perfectly capture in layperson's terminology the distinction between institutions and members of institutions, particularly in a relatively brief phone conversation with a stranger, but ours would seem to be a not-unreasonable attempt to get people to respond to the differences.

We hoped that the two different questions for each institution might distinguish between support for the regime and for the authorities, thus providing an empirical basis for a distinction about which previous scholars, like Easton, have only theorized in the most abstract fashion. The results are presented in Figure 3.1. Perhaps the most noticeable aspect of the figure is the low approval level for members of Congress as a group. Collapsing the "approve" and "strongly approve" responses, less than one-fourth of the respondents approved of members of Congress. Approval of George Bush at the time of the survey was 46 percent, and approval of the then-current members of the Supreme Court was a whopping 73 percent.

But a focus on the institution produces, by contrast, strongly positive feelings. About 95 percent of the public approves of the Supreme Court and the presidency as institutions, regardless of who is in office, and most notably, 88 percent of the public approves of the Congress as an institution. If we look specifically at those who strongly approve, 19 percent of the 1,409 valid respondents even gave very high approval ratings to Congress as an institution.[2]

It is clear that a drop-off is registered for all three bodies as attention

2 At the same time, this figure of only 19 percent strong approval indicates that the "institution" question is picking up something more than knee-jerk patriotic expressions of devotion to the constitutional structure itself.

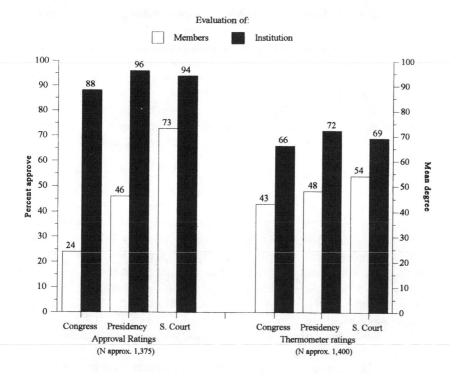

Figure 3.1. Evaluations of members and institutions

is directed away from the institution and toward the individual members – but the drop-off for Congress is of incredible magnitude. The Court witnesses the smallest drop, only 22 percentage points. Approval of George Bush is nearly 50 points lower than approval of the presidency. And approval of the members of Congress is 64 points lower than approval of Congress as an institution.

Results based on the feeling thermometer bear out the same general pattern of greater favorability toward the institutions than toward the members, although the range is more constrained than is the case with the simple approval question. As is well known, when presented with a 0-to-100 feeling-thermometer scale, many respondents are unable to resist the siren call of the 50-degree response. Even so, ratings of institutions are still much higher than ratings of their members and Congress continues as the lowest of the three institutions.

As an important aside, it should be noted that 67 percent of our respondents claim to approve of their own member of Congress. At the same time, the public dislikes the leaders of Congress; only 25 percent approves of them. This figure is nearly identical to that elicited when the referent is all members of Congress. This no doubt explains the initially surprising finding of Lipset and Schneider's experiment that asking about the job performance of the leaders of Congress and asking about the job performance of Congress generally produce very similar results (1987: 89–93). Whether the referent is leaders of Congress or all members of Congress matters little to the public. Both are perceived to be part of a largely undifferentiated group that is too often tainted by scandal and too seldom part of solutions to societal problems.

Support for Congress is not totally absent; it just tends to be directed at certain aspects of Congress. Further evidence of this point comes from several open-ended questions in our survey. Early in our survey instrument, after obtaining some routine level-of-interest information, we asked people if there was anything they liked or disliked about the federal government, and then if there was anything they liked or disliked about Congress. When asked to think of what they liked about Congress, 82 percent of the public was able to come up with something positive to say. Of course, to be fair, 88 percent were able to list something they disliked about Congress. But the point is that few individuals think Congress is without any redeeming value. People do not simply and viscerally hate Congress; they do not approve of the performance of the people in Congress, excepting their own member.

Significantly, when people are asked, as they often are these days, about their attitudes toward Congress with no further specification provided, they routinely report their attitudes toward the general membership of Congress. People almost always view Congress as the summation of its members, nothing more. Detailed confirmation of this is found in later chapters. People's tendency to equate the congressional membership with Congress has led political observers toward an erroneous interpretation that people unequivocally hate Congress. While this is understandable, and although popular displeasure with aspects of Congress is widespread, this conclusion is incomplete; people generally approve of the institution, and they generally disapprove of the membership.[3]

---

3 For purposes of comparison we asked respondents about two nonpolitical institutions: labor unions and big business. They received feeling-thermometer ratings well below all three political institutions, even Congress. The mean feeling-thermometer rating for labor unions was 49 and for big business 50, fifteen points lower than the mean feeling-thermometer rating for Congress, and about twenty below the presidency and the Supreme Court. Lipset and Schneider (1987) report on a broader battery of nonpolitical institutions.

WHY IS CONGRESS THE LEAST LIKED POLITICAL INSTITUTION?

The public is anything but totally enamored with the Supreme Court and the presidency. For example, only 38 percent of our survey respondents disagreed with the statement that the Supreme Court is involved in too many issues. Nearly 58 percent reported being upset with recent Court decisions. Even more people during the summer of 1992 – 62 percent – claimed to be upset by the president's recent policy decisions, and 59 percent did not agree with the statement that "recent presidents have led the country well." But no matter whether the focus is on individuals or the institution, approval ratings or feeling thermometers, Congress is ranked dead last among the three institutions. This fact, combined with the "confidence" findings covering the past twenty years, confirms that Congress has a problem in terms of public perceptions. But why is the public more upset with Congress than with the other branches?

For assistance in answering this question, we return to the distinction between policy concerns and process concerns. Are people upset with the legislation Congress passes or with how Congress goes about its business? Since we are interested here in a comparison among institutions, we must also determine whether people are that much happier with the policies advanced and processes employed by the Supreme Court and the presidency.

Likes and dislikes

In our survey, we asked respondents many more questions about Congress than about either the presidency or the Supreme Court, yet there are enough questions on the other institutions to permit comparisons. In each of our open-ended questions on people's likes and dislikes concerning the federal government and Congress, we probed for three responses. Respondents could therefore mention up to three things they liked about the federal government, three things they disliked, and so on. Responses were coded and then categorized as being primarily policy oriented, process oriented, person oriented, or miscellaneous (see Appendix), thus permitting a determination as to whether respondents focus on people in government, policy, or process when they think about their likes and dislikes of the federal government and Congress.

Table 3.1 shows what people mentioned in response to the open-ended questions. When asked what they like about the federal government, 40 percent mention policy and 32 percent mention process. When

Table 3.1. *Open-ended responses on likes and dislikes*
of the federal government and Congress

Category of response	Like fed. govt.	Dislike fed. govt.	Like Congress	Dislike Congress
People	6%	25%	32%	56%
Policy	40	45	6	7
Process	32	11	40	21
(Misc.)	(22)	(19)	(22)	(16)
Total number of responses	1,268	2,304	1,281	2,575

asked about their dislikes, policy-oriented responses increase slightly, to 45 percent, whereas process-oriented responses decrease to 11 percent. Clearly, the policies of the federal government are factors in people's attitudes toward it, much more than are processes and the people in government.

But contrast these results with those for Congress. When asked what they like about Congress, respondents usually mention process, with people in Congress coming in second. Positive comments about policy are almost nonexistent. Policy is also rarely mentioned by people when asked about their dislikes of Congress. Fully 56 percent of respondents mention the people in Congress when asked what they dislike about Congress, while 21 percent mention process.

Further insight into the public psyche is possible by subdividing the broad categories employed in Table 3.1. What is it about the federal government's processes that people like? Most often (35 percent), it is the general way the political system has been structured by the Constitution, though many respondents (21 percent) made favorable references to concepts such as representation and elections. Volunteered dislikes of federal-government processes tilted heavily toward over-bureaucratization (31 percent) and inefficiency (16 percent).

What about the composition of process responses concerning Congress? The high percentage of "like" mentions relating to process may seem at first glance to go against our claims that people are upset with processes, but these favorable responses tend to relate to representational and electoral ideals Congress can approximate (27 percent) and to the location of Congress in the overall system of checks and balances (18 percent). Dislikes of congressional process, however, commonly include references to inefficiency (30 percent), an unwillingness to work with the president (15 percent), and an unwillingness to work with other members of Congress (11 percent).

People like Congress's place in the constitutional system, and they like the potential of a body such as Congress to connect government to the people, but they do not like the way Congress goes about its work, associating it with inefficiency and a lack of cooperation. And on the whole, when thinking about the entire federal government, people often react to policy items, sometimes favorably and sometimes unfavorably. But when thinking about Congress, people rarely react to specific policies, perhaps because a single institution like Congress is seldom able to enact policies unilaterally.

Instead, to a much greater degree than with the federal government, people's reactions to Congress, whether positive or negative, are quite often process related. And even these figures may understate the centrality of process. We will argue later that a high percentage of the dislike mentions related to "people in Congress" is actually connected with process, as numerous respondents believe the people in Congress are a problem because of the system in which they must operate. People often like or dislike the federal government because of policies, and they often like or dislike Congress because of processes.

Ideological proximity

Even if people do not mention policy spontaneously when they think about Congress, they may still believe Congress is farther removed from their own policy and ideological orientations than the president or the Supreme Court. This could lead people to be dissatisfied with Congress. We asked the survey respondents to place themselves on a five-point ideology scale (liberal, slightly liberal, moderate, slightly conservative, and conservative). We also asked them to place Congress, George Bush, and the Supreme Court on the same scale. The mean ideology self-placement for respondents was 3.3, meaning they were generally moderate but leaning slightly toward the conservative side. Congress at the time was perceived to be more liberal than respondents, with a mean score of 2.5 (a difference of 0.8), whereas then-president Bush was seen to be more conservative than the people, with a mean score of 3.9 (a difference of 0.6). On average, people thought the Supreme Court was the closest to them ideologically, achieving a mean score of 3.6 (only 0.3 more conservative on a scale of 1 to 5).

These means, however, might hide real differences in the typical distance between an individual's own orientation and that of other actors.[4]

4 To illustrate the need for individual-level computations, consider the extreme case

Table 3.2. *Differences in ideological orientation
between self and the three branches*

Ideological difference	Self – Congress	Self – Bush	Self – S. Court
0	19%	25%	22%
1	19	24	23
2	26	26	27
3	17	12	13
4	19	13	15
	—	—	—
Total percent	100	100	100
N	1,108	1,239	1,116
Mean difference	2.0	1.7	1.8

It is more useful to note the gap for each person between, say, themselves and Congress. In other words, instead of the difference between mean locations, the real issue is the mean of the perceived differences at the individual level. We therefore created a difference scale that measures the distance between respondents' self-placement and that of Congress, Bush, and the Supreme Court. The perceived differences are reported in Table 3.2. On a scale of 0 to 4, where 0 represents no ideological difference and 4 represents the farthest distance possible, the mean differences across institutions are quite similar (2.0 points for Congress, 1.7 for then-president Bush, and 1.8 for the Supreme Court).[5]

While Congress is seen as the most distant ideologically from the views of the people, the key point is that it is only very slightly more distant from the people than the Supreme Court and the president. What is more, it is well known that people's ideological self-placement tends to be more conservative than their actual positions on issues such as the

where half the public identifies themselves as pure conservatives and identifies the Congress as pure liberals. The other half of the public claims to be pure liberals but feels Congress is solidly conservative. The mean ideological scores for self-placement and for placement of Congress would be identical, suggesting that the public felt ideologically close to Congress even though in actuality every person surveyed was as far from Congress as possible.

5 When placement means were used, the Supreme Court appeared very close to people's ideological self-placement (only 0.3 off), but when the preferable procedure is employed we discover that the public is very much like the other two institutions in the extent to which individual respondents view it as close to or far from their own ideological position.

government's provision of services. If we were computing distance from specific policies rather than broad ideologies, Congress may very well be closer to the public than are the other two institutions. Besides, the ideology of Congress, the Supreme Court, and especially the president changes over time, yet Congress is consistently the least liked institution, so it is unlikely that the explanation for this habitual dissatisfaction involves perceived distance on matters of ideological substance. The brevity of the increase in support for Congress after the Republican takeover in 1995 is further indication of this point.

Perceived institutional clout

Even though the public is not particularly agitated because of specific congressional policy decisions, or because it believes Congress to be out of step ideologically, this does not mean that Congress is believed to be substantively irrelevant. In fact, perhaps our biggest surprise in conducting this research was the discovery that people believe Congress is by far the most powerful institution of government. Why should this be surprising? Because countless astute observers of modern American politics believe the president has eclipsed Congress.

It seems to be required for introductory American politics texts to stress the power of the president. Anthony King writes that "the presidency of the U.S. is a grand office and one that has tended to get grander as the years have gone by" (1992: 1). Morris Fiorina is undoubtedly correct when he notes that "certainly on the national level most analysts have viewed the presidency as stronger than the Congress at least since the time of FDR" (1992: 79; see also 1988: 442). Perhaps due to this consensus of analysts, Fiorina's own research proceeds on the assumption that the people view the presidency as being more powerful than Congress. At one point, he suggests that the advantage of the presidency in clout was about 2 to 1 in 1980 and nearly 3 to 1 in 1984 (1988: 447).[6] We hear much talk of this being an "antiparliamentary" or "proexecutive" era in which the airwaves are dominated by the executive, in which complexity makes it difficult for generalist legislative bodies to cope, and in which rapid decisions are often needed in a dangerous, quickly changing, and interconnected world.

However strong this consensus of analysts, someone forgot to tell the American people that the presidency is more powerful than Congress. Consider the following. We asked respondents, "Which part of the gov-

6 Some confusion occasionally surfaces over whether the issue is the actual power ratio or the power ratio as perceived by ordinary people. Given Fiorina's purpose (to explain why voters act the way they do), perception of the power ratio is obviously the factor that matters.

ernment is most responsible for the massive budget deficits currently facing the U.S. government?" The three options provided were Congress, the presidency, or both. It seemed likely that people would gravitate toward the "both" response, which is an easy answer to give and probably reflects most accurately the situation. But the people think otherwise. Only about one out of four (27 percent) felt both institutions were responsible. One out of five (21 percent) felt the presidency was most responsible, leaving a remarkable 56 percent to register the belief that Congress was most responsible.

But this could be due to the notion that Congress possesses the power of the purse and is therefore abnormally powerful on an issue such as the budget deficit. Thus, a more appropriate approach is simply to ask the people if they believe each institution has too much power, about the right amount of power, or not enough power. When this is done, we find that, while the percentage of the public believing the Supreme Court and the presidency have too much power is relatively modest (26 and 19 percent respectively), a much more substantial 43 percent believe Congress has too much power. More people believe the presidency has not enough power than believe it has too much, but when attention turns to the Congress, nearly five times as many people believe it has too much power than not enough. Congress, by quite a hefty margin, is viewed to be too powerful an institution of the federal government.

It is easy to find confirmation of this conclusion from statements made during the focus-group sessions. In fact, before we had ever seen the results of our survey, the focus-group participants, by virtue of their near-unanimous perception that Congress was the most powerful institution, had sensitized us to this possibility. The following comment from a focus-group participant is not atypical: "I thought the president has become almost more of a monarchy. I mean the president is just more of a figurehead . . . no real decision-making of any lasting consequence is made by the president. It's just like, you know, look at the monarchy in England."

Perhaps the widespread public perception that Congress is the most powerful institution is an artifact of our research being conducted in 1992, a year in which President Bush was availing himself of many opportunities to campaign against a "do-nothing" Congress and the gridlock it created. As it turns out, people have been convinced for quite some time that Congress was the most powerful body. More than twenty years ago, Davidson and Parker (1972) and Dennis (1973), using different data, arrived separately at the conclusion that "Congress emerges as the institution perceived to have greatest impact upon people's lives" (Dennis, 1973: 12). The data they present are as supportive for the early

1970s as ours are for the early 1990s. People think Congress is more powerful and have believed this to be the case for quite some time.

What may have changed is support for the power of Congress. Dennis concluded that "Congress appears to have an edge over other institutions in the level of support for its power. Certainly my own recent data show this" (1973: 15). Donald Devine similarly noted that people prefer congressional power overwhelmingly to presidential power (1972: 158–163). As our results show, little support remains for the power of Congress. Nearly half of our respondents wanted Congress weakened and only 9 percent wanted it strengthened.

Be that as it may, it is unfortunate that the public's perception of congressional power has been so unappreciated by analysts, because this perception has extremely important implications and must be placed at the core of any serious attempt to come to grips with the reasons for public displeasure with the institution. It suggests that people hold Congress more responsible than the other institutions for societal problems. In this sense, part of the explanation for the fact that public unhappiness is most directly targeted at Congress is the belief that Congress has the most to do with current conditions. If citizens are upset with current economic conditions, why should they vent their spleens at institutions that they believe lack the power to affect significantly those conditions?

The people may be committed to having a legislative institution, but this does not mean they wish to imbue this institution with a great deal of power. The people value the balance-of-power concept (more on this later), and many believe the balance is currently out of whack not, as many political scientists believe, because of executive aggrandizement in a media-centered, complex, and dangerous era, but because of the inordinate power of Congress.

Valence dissatisfaction

It is time to make an important qualification in our argument. While we have been stressing process over policy as the primary explanation for public unrest with political institutions, we have done so because from our vantage point process factors have been so grossly understudied and underemphasized as contributors to the people's unhappiness. We do not believe policy is irrelevant to dissatisfaction. Indeed, the preceding section on the perceived clout of Congress compared to the presidency and the Supreme Court, and our belief that the resultant culpability of Congress is a factor in its unpopularity, points to the importance of policy.

Additional evidence is derived from our battery of questions on the

Table 3.3. *Handling of most important problem facing the nation*

Handling of job	Congress	Presidency	Supreme Court
Good	2%	8%	10%
Fair	23	30	45
Poor	75	62	46
N giving evaluation	1,354	1,366	710
(% of total N saying "doesn't deal with problem")	(2)	(2)	(44)

most important problem facing the country. Respondents' answers to the initial question are themselves interesting. Most people said the most important problem was economic in nature, with 13 percent specifically mentioning unemployment, 17 percent the deficit, and 21 percent the economy in general. The economy was definitely on people's minds in 1992. But relevant at this juncture are the follow-up questions we asked. Once respondents had indicated the most important problem facing the nation, we asked how good a job each institution was doing in dealing with the problem they mentioned: a good job, a fair job, or a poor job. The results are presented in Table 3.3.

Many respondents, 44 percent, recognize that the Supreme Court does not deal directly with some of the problems identified as "most important." This, we would argue, is part of the reason people like the Supreme Court best. People see the nation facing some big problems, but they do not believe the Supreme Court has anything to do with the problems. It is not that the Supreme Court is doing a bad job or a good job. Rather, the Supreme Court is irrelevant in these areas and therefore cannot feel the brunt of public anger when the problems are not solved.

But people are likely to believe that the president and Congress should be dealing with national problems, and they clearly think that neither the presidency nor the Congress has done a good job. Only 2 percent of respondents think Congress is doing a good job handling the most important problem facing the nation, and only 8 percent think the presidency is doing a good job. By far, most people think both the Congress and the presidency are not handling the problem. But here we see that people perceive Congress to be doing a worse job than the presidency. Three out of four respondents believe that Congress does a poor job dealing with the most important problem facing the nation. This is a powerful indictment of Congress. The presidency does not fare well, but Congress fares even worse.

Here again we see a form of policy dissatisfaction – failure to deal with the most important problem facing the country – and we would be surprised if this so-called policy dissatisfaction did not translate somehow into diminished institutional support. At the same time, it is crucial for us to distinguish the kind of policy dissatisfaction we have been describing with alternative ways of conceptualizing policy dissatisfaction. To the extent policy contributes to public unhappiness with Congress, it is not that the public is upset with a particular congressional action. It is more likely reflective of a belief that the country faces big problems and that Congress is not solving them. Many of us have grown accustomed to thinking of policy in Left/Right terms, but the public does surprisingly little of this. Unrest with what seemed in 1992 to be an almost permanently Democratic Congress, as we will see, is nearly as strong among the left-of-center public as it is among those right of center. This kind of policy dissatisfaction is not at the core of the situation, nor is it the kind that can be traced to a specific congressional policy misstep. Passing H.R. 1 when H.R. 2 should have been passed is, of course, unlikely to ruffle too many feathers.

Rather, it is the kind of policy dissatisfaction that springs from a sense that something should be happening but is not happening. This, in turn, could flow from heightened demands of a public that has increasingly come to believe it is entitled to receive from the federal government a certain quality of life, demands that are only fueled by politicians on both sides of the aisle when they encourage people to think that they can solve frustrating, intractable, important problems better and faster than the other side, as well as by the media's proclivity to call attention to, perhaps even to magnify, these problems.

This is what we call valence dissatisfaction, after the concept of valence issues – those issues for which the desired ends are not in question. Valence issues include such things as improving the economy and reducing crime, where virtually everyone supports the goal, thus confining potential disagreement to the means by which these ends can be achieved. The kind of policy dissatisfaction we picked up seems to parallel the concept of valence issues. Overwhelming sentiment exists that the government should "do something" about key problems, but the public often demurs from engaging in the crucial debate about the specific means by which something should be done. Who would complain if the government were perceived to have actually moved toward solutions? Only the most ardent libertarian given to sour grapes. But does the dissatisfaction flowing from inevitable failures on many fronts constitute policy dissatisfaction? We are willing to say that it does, if we

55

are permitted the caveat that it certainly is a different type of policy dissatisfaction than what is usually connoted by the phrase.

This discussion of valence dissatisfaction is relevant to our cross-institutional comparisons because some institutions, by their design, can be openly viewed in the process of failing to solve major societal problems. In this respect, policy and process concerns are joined at the hip. More specifically, in the U.S. political system, it is the president who most often sets the policy agenda. He makes clear what his policy concerns are, during the campaign and after, even if this is sometimes done in rather vague terms. The media give the president the "bully pulpit" from which to be heard; and perhaps most important, he speaks most often in one voice, the occasional cabinet dispute notwithstanding. Thus, the president is to some extent the policy-agenda focal point.

Congress, on the other hand, is not perceived by the public as actively setting the policy agenda. We rarely hear about "Congress" standing on a soap box declaring that it wants a certain policy initiative passed. When key members of Congress do so, they are most often met with opposition voices from within the same body. In essence, members of Congress disagree with other members. Most often, Congress is perceived to be reacting to presidential initiatives in a cacophonous and, in the end, unresponsive manner.

But if this is so, how can Congress be perceived as so much more powerful than the presidency? If the president to a great extent sets the policy agenda, then in what way does Congress have so much power? We can turn to the focus-group participants for our answer. They emphasized over and over again that the president was trying hard to get things done but that Congress would not let him. Congress was an extremely powerful obstacle to a relatively weak president. When asked which branch is the most powerful, one participant answered, "The Congress. They are the ones that the president and everybody else has to go to to get them to approve things. They've got to vote on it and they're torn between themselves. So the whole works is messed up right there. That's what causes all the problems."

Thus, congressional power does not emanate from the setting of policy agendas, but from its ability to block what the president wants. So when survey respondents are asked about the job the president and Congress are doing handling the most important problem facing the nation or their responsibility for the budget deficit, people are more likely to see the president as at least trying to do something. Just because people clamor for a separation-of-powers system does not mean they like it when the separate powers do not cooperate – and the nature of congressional procedures virtually dictates that it will be perceived as the least cooperative.

EMOTIONAL REACTIONS TO POLITICAL INSTITUTIONS

We have established so far that people make a distinction between the institutions and their members, consistently approve of Congress (both institution and members) the least and the Supreme Court the most, think Congress has more power than the other branches, and believe the president and, especially, Congress have done poorly addressing the most pressing national problems. In our discussions of people's feelings, we have used words like "disgusted" and "upset," but we have not yet investigated how people really feel about Congress, the president, or the Supreme Court. Having added specificity to our understanding of the objects of feelings, it is now time to add specificity to the feelings themselves.

For too long, students of political attitudes and behavior gave short shrift to the emotional content of politics. Only recently have political scientists begun to examine how emotional reactions to politics affect evaluations, decisions, and behavior (Conover & Feldman, 1986; Kuklinski et al., 1991; Marcus, 1988; Marcus & MacKuen, 1993; Marcus et al., 1995; Sullivan & Masters, 1988; Theiss-Morse, Marcus, & Sullivan, 1993). Emotional reactions affect how we think about certain things and the actions we take. They may also say something important about how people perceive what is going on around them.

Fortunately, we included in our survey a series of questions measuring people's emotional reactions to the members of Congress, the president, and the Supreme Court justices. The preface to the questions was, "Now I'd like to have you compare your feelings toward people in government – the Supreme Court justices, the president, and members of Congress." Five separate items followed: "Which group makes you feel the most angry . . . afraid . . . disgusted . . . uneasy . . . proud?"[7] The pattern of responses is presented in Table 3.4.

Several results stand out in this table. Not surprisingly, members of Congress come out first in all four negative emotions. Compared to both the president and the Supreme Court justices, members of Congress make people feel more angry, disgusted, afraid, and uneasy. Simply put, members of Congress generate a lot of negative emotions in the public.

7 We also recorded volunteered answers of "all" or "none." These answers highlight perhaps the most depressing feature of our analysis of emotional reactions. Respondents had few qualms in choosing one of the three institutions for the negative emotions. But this is not so when respondents were asked, "Which group makes you feel the most proud?" When all respondents are included (except those saying they don't know and those refusing to answer), 29 percent volunteered that none of the options made them feel the most proud. This response is a sad commentary on the state of positive emotional reactions to government institutions and their members.

Table 3.4. *Emotional reactions to members of Congress, the president,*
and the Supreme Court justices

Members of institutions	Angry	Disgusted	Afraid	Uneasy	Proud
Supreme Court justices	7%	7%	24%	20%	35%
Members of Congress	60	61	45	48	14
President	33	32	32	32	51
N	1,243	1,197	1,110	1,203	919

They also generate the least pride. Half of the people mentioning a particular institution said the president made them feel proud. This is not unusual in that the president serves as the symbol of our government in many regards. The Supreme Court justices also generate feelings of pride in a significant number of people. On this positive emotion, members of Congress come in a rather distant third.

Respondents are especially likely to feel anger and disgust toward Congress. About 60 percent of respondents chose members of Congress as generating these emotional reactions. The percentage drops to about 45 percent for afraid and uneasy. The Supreme Court justices, on the other hand, generate different emotional responses. Whereas only 7 percent of respondents say the justices make them feel angry or disgusted, 24 percent say they make them feel afraid, and 20 percent say they make them feel uneasy. The percentage of people choosing the president hovers just over 30 percent for all four negative emotions.

The reason for the institutional members generating different emotions in the public may in part be found in the institutions themselves. Congress does its work in the open. The public sees almost all of the dirty laundry – both the perceived inefficiency (such as the disagreements, the bickering, the haggling, the obstructions put before the president) and the perceived inequity (such as the alleged influence of special interests, and of selfish concerns on the part of members themselves [scandals, perquisites, and so on]). The public feels angry and disgusted at what it sees. The work of the Supreme Court, on the other hand, is done behind closed doors. The media occasionally report on a Supreme Court decision, but even then the public hears only the final summary judgment. What went on in private or even in the courtroom itself remains a mystery to all but a few Americans. This secretive and mysterious process is more likely to generate feelings of uneasiness and fear than anger and disgust. People are not sure what the Supreme Court is doing or what it will do next, but they know what Congress will do next, and they feel angry and disgusted about the whole thing. So the processes of the separate institutions may in fact feed into the emotional reactions people have toward the institutional membership.

POLITICAL INSTITUTIONS AND CONSTITUTIONAL STRUCTURE

The negative attitudes and emotional reactions discussed thus far seem targeted primarily toward the members of institutions or actions taken by those members. They should not be taken to mean that the public is highly displeased with the basic structure of the federal government. Among our survey respondents, 62 percent either feel neutral toward or disagree with the statement, "Only a very big change in our whole system of government will allow us to solve this country's problems." Moreover, 35 percent strongly approve of the "basic constitutional structure of the U.S. government," another 56 percent approve, while only 8 percent disapprove and only 9 respondents (0.6 percent) strongly disapprove.

Little sentiment exists for tinkering with institutional relationships currently enshrined in the Constitution even as people are quite unhappy with the way the political system is actually operating. To provide a more specific illustration of this attitude, we asked a long question on altering the power relationship of the president and Congress: "In the United States, Congress and the president share power. This keeps either branch from gaining too much power but sometimes stops anything from getting done. In most other countries of the world, the executive is stronger than the legislature, which means that the government is likely to get more done but the executive can become very powerful. Which do you prefer – the president and Congress sharing power or having the executive stronger?"

Despite our attempt to be even-handed in specifying the strengths and weaknesses of a political system embodying a firm notion of checks and balances, as well as one tending more toward a parliamentary arrangement of executive and legislative powers, there was a strong consensus answer to this query. More than 80 percent of the survey respondents support the current power-sharing arrangement, whereas less than 20 percent were attracted to the notion of a more powerful executive. Even though many people believe that Congress has too much power, little sentiment exists to change the system so that the executive would be significantly stronger in relation to Congress than is currently the case. People are quite willing to entertain changes in the political system, but they are unwilling to support changes that would cut to the heart of the Constitution and the relationship among major political institutions.

In a similar vein, we asked about people's preferences with regard to the convergence or divergence of party control of the Congress and the presidency. The public is split nearly down the middle on whether it is preferable for the country to have a president from the same political party that controls Congress. Slightly more than 42 percent prefer the president and the Congress to be of the same party, while 44 percent prefer divided government. The remaining 14 percent were so strongly partisan (presumably) that they would not answer, even after cajoling, without knowing which party would be in control of both branches.

We did not ask a specific question about support for a constitutional change that would eliminate the possibility of divided government, but given that 44 percent actually favor divided government, given the comments of the focus-group participants, and given the general reluctance to make major changes in the constitutional structure, we are confident that people would grant this proposal a chilly reception. The public is convinced that these problems with the polity do not require major constitutional manipulations.

AN ENEMY BECAUSE IT IS PUBLIC

On the basis of both our focus-group sessions and the survey responses, we believe an important element of distaste for Congress either has been missed altogether or at least underemphasized by previous investigators. To wit: Congress embodies practically everything Americans dislike about politics. It is large and therefore ponderous; it operates in a presidential system and is therefore independent and powerful; it is open and therefore disputes are played out for all to see; it is based on compromise and therefore reminds people of the disturbing fact that most issues do not have right answers. Much of what the public dislikes about Congress is endemic to what a legislature is. Its perceived inefficiencies and inequities are there for all to see.

Focus-group participants and survey respondents are disgusted by what they perceive to be undue interest-group influence in Congress. "Why doesn't Congress represent real people?" participants would ask. Again, part of Congress's problem is that perceived inequities are played out in public. People frequently see stories of members of Congress being too cozy with special interests, and they find such behavior disgusting. Moreover, when Congress does take action it is seldom fast. Madison believed this was good. He saw the Senate especially as protecting the people from themselves (Madison, 1964) and their oscillating moods and whims. But the public does not like overly deliberate politics. They would like to see something done quickly when in fact legislatures – particularly legislatures like the U.S. Congress – are not well-equipped for rapid action. Viewed in this context, it should be less than a shock that the public does not like Congress.

Thus, the very openness of the legislative process, which might otherwise be thought to endear Congress to the people, is much more likely to have the opposite effect. Nasty, visible disputes within the executive branch are fairly rare, and interest-group activity there is seldom reported. Occasionally, cabinet rivalries and leaked position papers give the general public a glimpse of maneuverings at the highest policy levels of the presidency, but such instances are infrequent. For the most part, proposals flow from the White House with apparent unanimity from those involved. Dissenters remain quiet or fall in line after the decision is made, in accord with the structure of a hierarchically organized entity. And the Supreme Court, of course, has been artful at camouflaging its disputes. The Court's "bickering" takes place behind carefully closed doors. Decisions, even when divided, are announced cleanly, and the public remains largely unaware of dissenting opinions. No open disputes, visible partisan stances, or transparent interest-group machinations can be seen. Decisions are presented as final products, not works in progress.

The public prefers some degree of certainty, and when there is not certainty the public wants to believe that disputes take place on the merits of the issues. The public, for the most part, does not like the partisan debates, competing interests, and compromises that many close observers of modern democratic politics believe are unavoidable. Congress is the institution in which these distasteful elements of politics are most readily visible. Thus, while Congress is sometimes viewed by the public as an enemy, we wish to call attention to the fact that it is often viewed as an enemy *because* it is so public.

4

Perceptions of congressional features and reforms

While no branch of government is without fault, the public's greatest disappointment is with Congress, the "first" institution. People view Congress as grossly inefficient and inequitable, but also as highly powerful. They believe members of Congress could be using their power for the good of the country, but instead use it for their own self-interested advantage. Given that most people like the institution of Congress very much, why do these same people believe the members of Congress are such an utter failure?

In this chapter, we begin to investigate the public's beliefs about what specifically is wrong with Congress, and in the next chapter we look at these beliefs in even greater depth. Stated simply, people think members of Congress have bought into the "Washington system," which seduces members away from fulfilling their responsibility to the public. Members of Congress are quickly corrupted by special interests and lobbyists, by the office perquisites they receive, and by the people who surround and indulge them. Once the public is convinced this has happened, members of Congress cannot do anything right. The various congressional scandals that hit the media simply provide proof that public judgment is correct. People think inefficiency and especially inequity reign supreme.

But are people's perceptions of the Washington system on target? Perhaps their hostility is in part an outgrowth of serious misperceptions of, for example, the perquisites members of Congress receive. Upon what knowledge do people base their judgment that members of Congress are dominated by the Washington system? And given the perceived problems of Congress, what, if anything, can be done to improve public perceptions? We look at recent calls for congressional reforms, especially term limitations, and find that these desired reforms seek to diminish the influence of the Washington scene on members of Congress. If members are unwilling or unable to resist the seduction of Washington, the public is very much in favor of forcing them to stay in touch with the people.

Perceptions of congressional features and reforms

Analyses of people's perceptions of specific congressional features and specific reform proposals form the core of this chapter.

WHAT IS THE "WASHINGTON SYSTEM"?

We asked our survey respondents the following question: "Do you think the wrong kind of people are running for Congress in the first place or do you think there is something about Congress that has a bad effect on people once they get into office?" While 21 percent believe the wrong kind of people run for Congress, 51 percent think Congress has a bad effect on people and another 26 percent think it is a combination of both bad people and something bad about Congress. Thus, 77 percent believe Congress pollutes the people elected to serve in it, regardless of whether those people were formerly good or already somewhat bad.

The focus-group participants were outspoken in support of this view as well. One participant said, "I really feel like it wouldn't matter if we were in Congress. I think we would more or less act just as they're acting. I think this is something you fall into." She went on to say, "You find so many good people going in and the next thing you know they're corrupted." These sentiments dovetail with the widely publicized comments of former presidential candidate Ross Perot, and the confluence may help explain Perot's surprising popularity: "Take any good, decent citizen, give him enough perks, privilege, and access, and he'll lose touch with reality" (as quoted in Wilentz, 1993: 35).

But what is it about Washington that produces these negative perceptions? We asked the survey respondents whether they agreed, disagreed, or were neutral toward a battery of questions about Congress and its members. Their responses are presented in Table 4.1. On the basis of these responses and related information, we can begin to unravel what it is about Washington that the public thinks is so poisonous. These perceived features include the power of "special interests" in Washington, the city's insularity and resultant inattention to both local and national interests, and its perquisite-dominated structure.

Special interests

Weighing most heavily on the public's mind is the influence of special interests. People believe wholeheartedly that interest groups have too much influence over members of Congress. An astounding 86 percent of respondents believe Congress is too heavily influenced by interest groups. But what does the phrase "interest group" connote to most respondents? Whereas close observers of politics are likely to see interest groups as vital links between the public and the government, helping to capture

63

Table 4.1. *Opinions about Congress and the Washington system*

Statements	Agree	Disagree	Neutral
Congress does a good job representing the diverse interests of Americans, whether black or white, rich or poor.	30%	57%	13%
Congress addresses difficult issues in a reasonably efficient way.	25	64	11
Congress is too far removed from ordinary people.	78	15	7
Congress is too heavily influenced by interest groups when making decisions.	86	8	6
Just a few members of Congress have all the power.	43	47	10
Members of Congress focus too much on events in Washington.	70	16	14
Members of Congress come back to their districts too often.	9	78	13
Members of Congress are too sensitive to what the public-opinion polls tell them their constituents want.	45	44	11
Members of Congress should do what is best for the entire country, not just their district.	85	9	6
Members of Congress should do what their district wants them to do even if they think it is a bad idea.	49	41	10

Note: Number of cases for each question is approximately 1,400.

and to express the diversity of the public's views, the people themselves see the situation quite differently. Interest groups, they contend, are definitely not connected with ordinary people, even remotely. Instead, the popular notion is that these special interests are completely divorced from the public interest. The notion that special interests are actually working on behalf of the interests of some perfectly legitimate subset of the population is foreign to a surprisingly high percentage of people.

Interest groups may be of the Left or of the Right, but the perception is that they are not of the people. Left–Right distinctions are seldom noted by the average citizen, certainly less than they are by close political observers. In fact, for us, one of the more surprising features of the public mood is that people view special interests as largely monolithic even though casual observation often reveals special interests pitched in feverish battle with each other. Many ordinary citizens believe people like them are on the outside looking in while a cabal of high-powered interest groups successfully co-opts the process. They see interest groups as part of the Washington system, composed of individuals able and willing to play the political game and, therefore, able to extract more from the political system than they deserve.

The result is the perception that the interests of middle America are ignored in favor of greedy special interests. One focus-group participant said, "Unfortunately I think that Congress has reached a point now where . . . there are so many special-interest groups that have bucks, and [members of Congress] are going to work on taking care of them. The people that make the most noise get the most attention, and those people have the money and the numbers to get it." Another participant said that members of Congress "are so involved in all of these special interests, they can't even think for themselves anymore."

With these sentiments in mind, it is easy to understand how nearly 70 percent of respondents (those who are neutral or disagree) are unwilling to agree that Congress does a good job representing the diverse interests of Americans and still maintain that Congress is overly responsive to special interests. In their minds, special interests are not diverse. It is also easy to understand how 78 percent believe Congress is too far removed from ordinary people. People do not see interest groups representing ordinary interests but rather the interests of a very small, narrow, powerful group of people.

The political class often fails to appreciate the extent to which the public has an "us versus them" attitude – and the "them" is not Democrats or Republicans but anyone who plays a part in the Washington system: interest groups, political parties, the media, and politicians themselves. Both our national survey and our focus-group sessions indicate clearly that these attitudes are not confined to some marginalized, populist fringe. E. J. Dionne's fascinating account of divisions in the American Left and Right, as noted in Chapter 1, says little about why Americans hate politics. They hate the notion that there are insiders of any stripe. It reminds them of their own outsider status and it opens the possibility that benefits will be distributed in something other than a just and equitable fashion.

Washington, national, and constituent interests

The respondents also believe members of Congress are too fixated on events in Washington, but at the same time they think that members should do what is best for the entire country, not just their district. Does this make sense? It does, if we are careful to bear in mind what the phrase "Washington events" means to most respondents. The impression is sometimes given in scholarly writings that, since the public complains about their representative "going Washington" or catching "Potomac fever," they must want members to ignore national and international issues in favor of local ones. This is not true.

The public has no trouble with its representative being involved in important national issues. They clearly want their member to act on behalf of the country (85 percent), not the district (9 percent).[1] But they do not want their member to become embroiled in all the events swirling around Washington: the socializing, the fundraising, the junkets, the circuit. Participation in these events, and not a serious interest in national issues, is mainly what the public sees as "going Washington." Given this view, there is nothing inconsistent in coupling the desire for a national focus with the complaint that members of Congress are too involved with Washington events. The people want their representative to go to Washington and be involved with national events, not become immersed in the social scene.

What about the interests of constituents? Should members of Congress listen to the people of their districts? The public has mixed feelings on this topic: 49 percent think members of Congress should do what their district wants them to do even if they think it is a bad idea, while 41 percent disagree and another 10 percent are not sure. Similarly, 45 percent believe members of Congress are too sensitive to what the public-opinion polls tell them their constituents want, while 44 percent disagree and 11 percent are neutral. It should be noted that the latter statement associates public-opinion polls with constituent wishes – a connection the people prefer to disavow. They dislike the polls but like the notion of members paying attention to constituent views, so the resulting split verdict may be a natural consequence of the juxtaposition of a favorable and an unfavorable referent.

Even so, the public is clearly expressing some ambivalence about the extent to which ordinary people should influence policy decisions. They want members to pay attention to them, but this is not necessarily the

1 What, then, about pork-barrel projects? Many members of Congress devote significant energy to bringing home the pork. While constituents undoubtedly appreciate these efforts, pork is not nearly as important to them as might be imagined, or at least this is what they claim. When we asked respondents a series of questions on what they believed was the most important part of a representative's job, they mentioned two tasks most often: passing laws on important national problems and helping people deal with the governmental bureaucracy. Dead last in the list was bringing money or projects back to the district. We also asked, "To help balance the budget, would you encourage your representative to quit trying to bring federal projects back to your district even if other representatives around the country did not quit?" We thought this to be a stern test since the public was being asked if they were willing to give up unilaterally the race for pork. Even so, the answer was usually yes (55 percent). Constituents may be less parochial than is usually believed.

same as wanting members to take roll-call cues from them on every issue. The people want problems to be solved but are not much in the mood for playing a hands-on role in working through possible solutions (more on this shortly). In other words, the public believes members should pay attention to their constituents but should not look to the district for signals on how to act at every juncture. Members should be solicitous but they should not expect specifics. A possible explanation for this reluctance to have members of Congress look to the district for policy decisions emerges clearly from the focus groups.

Indeed, a surprising aspect of the focus-group sessions was the extent to which participants were self-deprecatory. Participants willingly and repeatedly blamed themselves for many of the problems in the political system today. People readily accept their own limitations, especially when it comes to knowledge about politics and political issues. As a result, a surprising number of people are anxious to defer to politicians on many issues – but they are kept from relaxing by the aforementioned ability of special interests to keep politicians from acting in the public interest. People are eager to have little to do with the political process, but they want to be sure their views would be taken seriously if they made the effort – and they also want to be sure the views of special interests are not given more weight than they deserve. People recognize that their partial disengagement from the political system has left them vulnerable, and they do not like the feeling.

Special perks

The survey respondents, and especially the focus-group participants, think members of Congress get too many special perquisites for being in office, and they mince few words in expressing their displeasure with the situation. One focus-group participant said, "They're given so much, and they have chauffeurs. I mean, they're treated like royalty." Another said, "They lose track of reality. . . . Free haircuts. Free lunch. They've got a free dining room. They get their free dry cleaning. I mean they just lose all sense of reality." In the public's view, the perquisites members of Congress are thought to receive are an integral part of the Washington scene.

Mentioned prominently by survey respondents as well as in press accounts and our focus-group discussions is the perception that members of Congress have a coterie of doting staffers and an all too attractive salary/pension package. Three of four respondents agreed with the statement, "There are too many staffers in Congress." Only 10 percent disagreed, and 15 percent were neutral. With remarkably little dissent, the public is not convinced members of Congress need the number of assistants they are perceived to have at hand. A parallel situation is present with regard to the financial remuneration of members of Congress. We asked respondents, "Do you favor or oppose reducing the salary for members of Congress?" Seventy-seven percent said they favored pay reductions. Having too many staffers and such high salaries, citizens fear, only encourages members to be swept up in the Washington system and to "lose all sense of reality."

Out of touch with ordinary people

So, members of Congress are overly influenced by interest groups, they pay too much attention to what is happening in Washington, and they care too much for the special perks they receive in office. The overall result is that they lose touch with ordinary people. We asked respondents if the president was closer to ordinary people than Congress, expecting to hear that the president was not – if for no other reason than the logistical difficulties of a single individual representing the diverse views of 270 million people. But instead, a surprising number of respondents answered yes, that the president is in fact closer to ordinary people (38 percent) or that Congress and the president were equally close (10 percent). In other words, about half the population does not believe Congress, the people's branch, is closer to the people.

This finding fits with the response that "Congress is too far removed from ordinary people" (78 percent), as well as with many comments made in the focus-group sessions. It would appear that not many people believe Congress is appropriately in touch with the public it serves. This is startling in that one of the presumed strengths of a legislative body is its ability to stay in touch with the people. Moreover, modern members of Congress make quite an effort to stay in touch with the people. Though the number of trips they take back to the district has dropped somewhat since its peak in 1980 (Hibbing, 1991), most members still maintain a withering pace of travel back to the district. They work hard at attending local events and visiting constituents. But the public does not see it this way. They want their member to come back to the district more often, indeed as often as possible. Only 9 percent thought members returned to the district often enough. Most wanted more attention devoted to the home fires.

How can constituents perceive Congress to be badly out of touch if members work so hard to stay in touch? The best answer we can provide comes from the focus groups. When information was provided to participants about congressional attempts to stay in touch, the most common retort was that these efforts seemed somewhat superficial.

Table 4.2. *Events contributing to dislike of Congress*

Event	A great deal	Some	Little/ not at all
Pay raise	77%	15%	8%
Thomas--Hill hearing	61	20	19
House bank scandal	78	14	8
Deficit gridlock	76	19	5

Note: Number of cases for each question is approximately 1,100.

Attending weddings and Fourth of July parades back in the district is apparently not what the people have in mind by "staying in touch." What respondents want is for members of Congress to come back to their district whenever possible to talk to real people, primarily so members will keep their feet on the ground and not be swept away by the Washington life. One focus-group participant suggested, "Maybe they need to spend a little more time in their district, and less time in Washington, DC, to get a feel for things."

In essence, members should come home frequently to immerse themselves in the values held by people in the district, they should like the district and its people, and they should listen not necessarily to specific policy preferences but more generally to the values and concerns of constituents. More important, the member should do so because he or she prefers the district, with its real people and ordinary life, to the surreal, influence-peddling, glitzy world of the nation's capital. At bottom, people do not want to be taken for granted.

SPECIFIC CONGRESSIONAL MISSTEPS

We asked our national sample about the extent to which four events contributed to their negative feelings toward Congress (those 311 respondents expressing no negative feelings toward Congress were excluded from this portion of the analysis). The results are presented in Table 4.2. As we mentioned earlier, the public thinks that the salaries of members of Congress are much too high. It is not surprising, then, that the public did not take kindly to the Senate deciding in 1991 to raise its salary to $125,000, which brought it in line with the salary of representatives. Even though in the same action senators agreed to ban

69

money made from honoraria and the like, the debate thrust congressional pay concerns into the national spotlight and was a sore point for many people.

Certainly it was a sore point for our respondents, as 77 percent felt the pay-raise incident contributed to their own negative feelings toward Congress. One focus-group participant summed up these feelings well. When asked what Congress should be doing, she said, "Well, I think for starters they wouldn't be voting themselves incredible pay raises when the rest of the country is taking pay cuts or layoffs. This, I think, was a slap in the face, a direct slap in the face to every American that has a job, or wants a job and doesn't have a job."

Also in 1991, Congress again found itself on the defensive over the manner in which it handled the confirmation hearings of Judge Clarence Thomas, who had been nominated by President Bush for a vacancy on the Supreme Court. Charges of sexual harassment against Judge Thomas were made by Professor Anita Hill. In the eyes of many, the all-male Senate Judiciary Committee was out of its element in understanding the charges and the proper manner to investigate them. A focus-group participant poignantly made the argument: "They don't understand anything that is important to me. And you saw that in the Anita Hill-Clarence Thomas hearings. Those guys had no idea what sexual harassment is. They all went 'What, what's that? You mean you don't like it when we squeeze your butt in the office?' And you know, that's where it said to me these guys have no idea what goes on in my life." People, supporters and opponents of Judge Thomas alike, also held the widespread perception that Congress did not handle the situation with aplomb. In fact, to many people the senators looked ridiculous. While mentioned least often as a source of negative feelings among our survey respondents, even here more than 60 percent said this event contributed a great deal to their negative perceptions of Congress.

Then Congress was rocked by another embarrassing situation in early 1992 when it became public knowledge that many members of the House were writing checks on accounts in the House bank even though there were insufficient funds in their accounts. Money would be placed in the account on the next payday, but it was clear that a large number of members were, in effect, kiting checks. The public was upset over what appeared to be another special privilege of serving in Congress. Many members decided to retire when lists of House bank abusers were made public. Several others were defeated in primary elections, and a few lost in the general elections some months later (see Ahuja et al., 1994).

The public was definitely not happy with what they perceived to be an abuse of power. Among the survey respondents, 78 percent said that the House bank scandal contributed a great deal to their negative feelings toward Congress. The focus-group participants felt the same way. One said, "I think Congress . . . has gotten too big for their britches. They got used to all the freebies, the perks, the nice things that come to them, the power, and it's just become taken for granted. It's become abused. Case in point – the checks, the bank scandal." The key point here is not whether members of Congress were actually doing something wrong, but that many people saw the bank scandal as another illustration of what was wrong with Congress. Insulated by a cushion of special provisions, members of Congress would have difficulty empathizing with ordinary people.

Finally, though it is more of a long-term problem than an isolated event, the difficult time Congress has had in attempting to solve the budget deficit has also been cause for public alarm. This alarm became loudest in late 1990 when President Bush and the Democratic Congress were seriously gridlocked over how to proceed: Bush trying to protect the defense budget and Congress more interested in shielding domestic spending. A failed summit agreement and a government closing parts of itself down in light of an expired temporary spending bill served as apt symbols of a system that was not working (and seemed to take public distaste for Congress to new depths). Even after these events, the massive deficit is a nearly constant reminder of congressional failures and quite likely fuels negative public feelings. Indeed, 76 percent of survey respondents said it contributed a great deal to their negative feelings toward Congress.

But the budget deficit is an enormous problem for the government to remedy. Does the public cut Congress any slack? The answer is basically no. In the public's eyes, the members are festooned with undeserved privileges and perquisites, consumed with desires for their own personal financial welfare, diverted by a welter of social events, and beholden to powerful denizens of the Washington special-interest network. A group so far out of touch with what they should be doing is never going to find success in the admittedly difficult task of reducing the deficit, the public believes.

ARE PEOPLE MISINFORMED ABOUT CONGRESS?

Now that we have a reasonably detailed outline of what people dislike about Congress, we can address issues concerning why people feel the way they do and what they would like to do to improve Congress. As to why the public has these negative perceptions, one possibility is that citizens have been misinformed and that what they really dislike is a caricature of Congress created by, among others, ribald radio talk-show hosts. If citizens could be told the facts of Congress, they would be much more supportive.

At least, this is common sentiment on Capitol Hill. Consider the comments of William Goodling (R.-Penn.): "If we [members of Congress] have a real shortcoming, it's in the area of educating the populace." Specifically, Goodling, along with colleague Peter J. Visclosky (D.-Ind.), thinks the public is especially misinformed about the perquisites and benefits members receive. "I've gotten letters saying we get free food, we get free haircuts. . . . People write half-truths, and all of a sudden it becomes gospel" (quoted in Duncan, 1991: 3554). As Alan Ehrenhalt notes, "Every conference on the subject of legislatures and their future includes at least one impassioned plea from an elected official to his colleagues to do a better job of educating reporters on the way legislatures work" (1992: 32).

The public is unquestionably misinformed about many aspects of Congress. Some of these faulty beliefs undoubtedly harm the institution. But our evidence suggests it would be a mistake to conclude that providing people with additional information would improve their attitudes toward the body. We asked survey respondents if they thought members of Congress had too many staffers and if they thought members should have their salaries reduced. Respondents overwhelmingly agreed with these sentiments: members of Congress do not need so many staffers nor should they be making as much money as they do.

But what if, for example, the public widely overestimates how many staffers members of Congress have? Maybe the public's desire to cut staff is based on the perception that members have more staffers than they really do. If this were the case, people could simply be informed of the true number of staffers and all would be well. Alas, the situation is quite the opposite. The public does misperceive the number of staffers per member, but people think there are fewer staffers, not more, than there actually are.

We asked respondents to tell us "on average, how many assistants or staff members does each member of the House of Representatives have?" The respondents' median estimate of the number of staffers per House member was 7.5 when the actual figure (for personal staffers only) in the 102d Congress was 17.4. Only 336 respondents thought members of the House had more personal staff than they really do, while fully 1,082 thought they had fewer. While the new Republican majority of the 104th Congress cut some committee staff, no reductions at all were made in personal staff, so this situation remains unchanged.

So, as far as staffing is concerned, informing the public would not diminish negative feelings toward Congress. In fact, if we were able to disseminate widely the true number of personal staffers each member is in a position to hire, the public would presumably be even more distressed by the staffing situation. The public thinks members have less than half the staff they actually possess, and they think that is too many. Imagine what this same public would feel if it knew the facts. Additional information about the number of staffers common in other national legislatures around the world would only exacerbate this situation, as the U.S. Congress is far and away the best-staffed legislature in the world. Further information on the constituency-service-oriented tasks of congressional staff and the different role of Congress in our system compared to most other national legislatures could ameliorate this same unrest, though probably not by much.

We also asked respondents to tell us their estimate of the annual salary (in 1992) of members of the House. What exactly did they think was too high? The median response to our question was $99,000. The actual figure at the time was $129,500. More people thought members made $75,000 or less (in other words, underestimated by $55,000 or more) than thought they made $129,500 or more. Of the 1,044 respondents willing to give a figure on how much they thought members of the House made, just 210 (20 percent) overestimated while 834 (80 percent) underestimated. Additional information on congressional pay would only make matters worse for people anxious to avoid a salary cut for members of Congress.

And of course none of this says anything about the other remuneration associated with being a member of Congress. We did not ask specific questions about each of the many perquisites of office available to members, but it was clear from the focus groups that the public is deeply disturbed by these perquisites – and that, as Representative Goodling suggests, much confusion exists over the specifics of these perquisites. For example, the public is aware that members of Congress are provided with a generous pension plan but they have no idea how it works. Some focus-group participants believed the same benefits were available to all former members regardless of how long they had been in Congress. The truth is that level of benefits is keyed to the highest three salaried years as well as to the number of years of service, with a ceiling of 75 percent of the highest salaried years. Those who stay a very short time draw practically nothing, but for careerists the plan is quite lucrative. And other misconceptions were common, such as the belief that each member is provided with a car and a driver.

Clearing up the public's common misperceptions about the rewards of serving in Congress might improve attitudes toward Congress, but we must caution against the expectation that this additional information would do much in the way of reversing negative perceptions. For starters, as we have seen, in at least two important instances – staff support and member salaries – the public believes members receive fewer rewards than they actually do. In these cases and no doubt in others, correcting misperceptions would only make matters worse. More generally, after listening to Americans both extensively and intensively, we are convinced that if the people were provided with a perfectly accurate accounting of member benefits they would still be, to put it mildly, quite disturbed, and they would still feel the package was too generous.

Misperceptions do exist, but correcting them would do little to reverse opinions of Congress. There is a larger problem that cannot be solved by making sure the public knows how many staffers a member is allowed and how the pension plan works. The problem is that the public thinks it sees members of Congress making decisions in an inefficient and inequitable manner – and being treated well in spite of their torpid performance. Correcting misunderstandings over just how well they are treated fails to address the core problem, especially since in some instances the members are treated better than the public thinks. We do not mean to imply that educating people about how members of Congress spend their day, the amount of time they put into casework for their constituents, and the amount of time they spend in their district would not help. In fact, we think it would. But the few questions we did ask on rewards of service clearly show that people's evaluations of Congress are often based on misperceptions, but not in the direction most often expected.

We did ask one more set of questions that is relevant to this discussion and that leads into our discussion of reforms. The public is enthusiastically supportive of term limits, but this support may be the product of a grossly overblown impression of how long typical members stay in Congress. Numerous focus-group participants talked about how members of Congress "have it so good" in Washington, with all of the perks and the money from special interests, that they never want to leave. Maybe if people were aware of actual levels of tenure and turnover, their support for term limits would wane.

Then again, maybe not. Support for congressional term limits has consistently been running at 70 percent or above. Our respondents were just as supportive of the idea, maybe more so. Nearly 80 percent wanted to limit the number of terms for members of Congress; 16 percent opposed the reform; and 4 percent did not know. The median length of service for members of the House in the 102d Congress was eleven years, so four out of five adults in the country think eleven years in the House is too long? Actually, they think eight years is too long. This figure is the median perception of House service length according to the 1,138 respondents in our sample answering this question. Only 21 percent

Table 4.3. *Support for proposed reforms*

Reforms	Support	Oppose	Don't know
Lengthen term of representatives	38%	58%	5%
Balanced-budget amendment	89	7	3
Reduce salary of members of Congress	71	22	7
Limit terms of representatives	80	16	4

Note: Number of cases for each question is approximately 1,350.

thought the mean length of service was more than twelve years – in other words, was clearly higher than the actual figure. On the basis of our sample, it would appear that, if anything, people underestimate the length of time the typical member has been in Congress, yet still support term limits. So once more we find a situation, parallel to that for salaries and staffers, where informing the public about life in Washington would not improve its perceptions of Congress.

CONGRESSIONAL REFORMS

If providing additional information about Congress is not the best strategy to improve public perceptions, perhaps enacting selected reforms is. The problems in Washington may be so deep that people believe only serious reform will do the trick. Indeed, reforms could decrease the perceived influence of the Washington system on Congress. Respondents were asked for their reactions to four reforms currently being discussed in some quarters of the polity: lengthening the term served by members of the House from two to four years; requiring that the federal budget be balanced; reducing the salary for members of Congress; and limiting the number of terms someone can serve in Congress. Summary measures of public sentiments are reported in Table 4.3 (see also Princeton Survey Research Associates, 1994).

The only reform in Table 4.3 opposed by a majority of the respondents is lengthening the term of U.S. Representatives. Little support (only 38 percent) exists for increasing the length of term to four years. Many analysts have argued that such a change would lessen the tendency of representatives to be driven by a concern for their own reelection. But giving members two extra years in Washington before they come up for reelection hardly wins many public hearts. Two extra years simply gives members of Congress more time to wallow in Washington life and diminishes their motivation to pay attention to the home folks.

But Table 4.3 also demonstrates the overwhelming public support of other proposed reforms. Nearly nine of ten American adults favor a balanced-budget amendment. A number of focus-group participants invoked the common line that since they have to balance their own family budget, members of Congress should balance that of the government. But other reforms receive nearly as much support. About 8 of 10 people wish to limit the number of terms people can stay in Congress, and more than 7 of 10 wish to reduce members' salaries. (We did not ask specifically about reducing the number of staffers and perquisites of the job, but it is apparent that these reforms would also be very popular with the public.)

All three of these highly popular reforms share a similar characteristic: they would all potentially force members of Congress not to become absorbed by Washington. A balanced-budget amendment would force members to make the hard choices (as balanced-budget requirements do for most Americans) and not allow members to give in to special interests (a major cause of budget problems, according to many citizens). Reduced salaries would mean that members of Congress could not as easily lose touch with the trials and tribulations of average working-class Americans. Term limits would mean that the lures of Washington, the perks and the money, could not have a permanent hold on anyone elected. We believe that these reforms would improve the standing of Congress in the minds of the people, though a substantial residue of dissatisfaction would remain, and though the improved level of public support might carry the price of undesirable consequences for the internal operations of Congress.

Term limits

We devote special attention to the movement to limit congressional terms because, as of this writing, it is the one of the four that has in some ways become a reality. The Senate has applied the brakes each time members of the House attempt to lengthen their terms (some senators are unwilling to set up a situation in which representatives can run for Senate seats without giving up the security of their House seats). It is highly unlikely that congressional salaries will actually be cut. In fact, cost-of-living increases now occur without the embarrassment of congressional votes. Adoption of a balanced-budget amendment is certainly not outside the realm of possibility. Such an amendment did not pass both houses of Congress, although even if it did, ratification by the states would be a long and uncertain process.

But after a fashion, term limits were an actual part of the political scene, if only temporarily. Oklahoma, Colorado, and California, in 1990, all limited the number of terms their state legislators could serve, but Colorado took the bold, and constitutionally suspect, step of also limiting the number of terms their members of Congress could serve (twelve years in both the House and Senate). Fourteen additional states followed Colorado's lead in the 1992 elections and six more did so in 1994. Term limits for national legislators did not fail in a single state where they were on the ballot in 1992 or 1994 and usually won by whopping margins. In the 103d Congress, 181 members (House and Senate combined) were operating under term limits ranging from six to twelve years in the House and always twelve years in the Senate. Unless the Supreme Court rules in the summer of 1995 that states do not have the right to impose such limitations on the pool of individuals eligible to serve in Congress (a distinct possibility), some members will actually be forced from the House in the late 1990s. Even if the Court throws out the state statutes, the leadership of Congress has promised a vote on a proposed constitutional amendment. Regardless of how all this plays out, the issue is fascinating from a philosophical point of view, and it will be with us for some time. So term limitation, besides being the most discussed reform, is also the most real.

In Chapter 6, we will investigate the type of individual most likely to support term limits, but for now background information is in order. First, the public's fondness for limiting terms does not stop with the legislative branch. Lest members of Congress feel the public is picking on them, we should note that the people support term limits for presidents and for Supreme Court justices just about as strongly as they do for members of Congress. When we asked if respondents favored or opposed limiting the term served by Supreme Court justices instead of allowing them to serve for life, 74 percent said they were in favor of limiting judicial terms for the highest court in the land. When we asked if presidents should be allowed to run for a third term, 70 percent of respondents said "no." These figures are quite similar to the level of support for congressional term limits uncovered in most surveys on the topic. The public is in favor not just of legislative term limits, but of political term limits of all stripes and apparently for all offices – legislative, judicial, and executive. People believe no one should be allowed to stay in Washington too long, but we focus our attention for now on public support for congressional term limits.

We are persuaded by Daniel Yankelovich of the usefulness of the concept of "public judgment." Yankelovich distinguishes between "people's top-of-the-mind offhand views (mass opinion) and their thoughtful, considered judgment (public judgment)" (1991: xii). To illustrate, Yankelovich contrasts public responses to abortion and to trade restrictions. He notes that most people have come to judgment on abortion as indicated by the fact that the introduction of new information or even new technologies does little to alter their views.

But with regard to protectionist trade proposals, new information makes all the difference to many respondents. Yankelovich cites an NBC/*Wall Street Journal* poll in which a 51 percent majority favored "greater limits on goods imported into the United States." But he proceeds to note that this figure dropped to 41 percent when it was mentioned that such legislation might restrict the variety and choice of products available; to 36 percent when people were told they might have to pay more for products; and to 19 percent when the possibility was raised that they might conceivably have to sacrifice quality in products (1991: 24–28).

Convinced that Yankelovich describes an important difference in public sentiments across issues, we included in our survey instrument an admittedly crude set of questions designed to provide some guidance on the matter of the extent to which the public had come to judgment on term limits. Are attitudes toward limits altered appreciably with the addition of information about possible consequences of the reform, or has the public come to a stable and informed judgment on the matter? Figure 4.1 provides the results of our attempt to answer this question. It reports the number of respondents favoring and opposing term limits for members of Congress, undecideds and nonrespondents excluded.

As we have already noted, the public is quite lopsided in favor of limiting terms. This fits with our earlier description of the public's disaffection with the Washington scene and its influence peddling, cocktail parties, and perquisites all conspiring to cause members to lose touch with ordinary people. A natural corollary of the belief that the Washington scene corrupts members is the belief that the longer members are exposed to that scene the more corrupted they will become. Term limits would make it impossible for members to get too far out of touch by limiting the length of time members could hold a particular office in Washington.

After obtaining these initial sentiments on term limits, we confronted the respondents with two contrary arguments. For those claiming to favor term limits, the first follow-up was, "Some people opposed to term limitations have suggested that the problems Congress deals with are so complex that it takes years for members of Congress to develop the expertise needed to address those problems." The second was, "Other

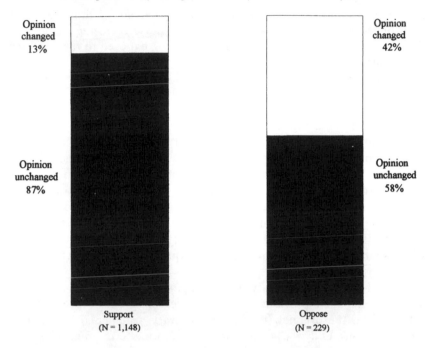

Figure 4.1. Public judgments on term limits

people opposed to term limitations have suggested that limiting terms for members of Congress would only increase the power of unelected staff members and interest group lobbyists." For those few souls opposing term limits, we also presented two contrary arguments. First, "Some people in favor of term limitations are concerned that current members of Congress, who win better than 95 percent of the time, don't give other people the chance to get into office." Second, "Other people in favor of term limitations have suggested that the longer representatives are in Congress the more they are influenced by the Washington interest-group scene."

After each probe, we asked if the respondents had thought at all about the contrary argument, then we asked, "Being aware of this argument, would you still favor (oppose) limiting the number of terms someone can serve in Congress?" Regardless of whether respondents support or oppose term limits, a surprising number admit they have not considered at least one and usually both of the contrary arguments (65 percent of those favoring term limits and 58 percent of those opposing term limits). The difference between supporters and opponents, however, in their willingness to change opinions in light of the contrary arguments is quite amazing: as indicated in Figure 4.1, only 13 percent of those favoring term limits, but a substantial 42 percent of those opposing them, said that they had changed their opinion after being exposed to the contrary arguments.

All told, 242 of the 1,377 respondents taking a position on term limits changed their minds. Put differently, nearly 18 percent of all eligible respondents could be talked out of their positions without a great deal of effort. So has the public come to judgment on term limits? Not totally. If Yankelovich's examples of abortion and trade restrictions constitute the poles of public judgment and "top-of-the-head" opinion respectively, it would appear that congressional term limitation as an issue is somewhere in the middle. The introduction of new information on the possible consequences of the proposal leads to just short of one out of five people changing their minds. Thus, the stability and certitude of judgment found in abortion attitudes is not present, but neither is the wild oscillation found in the battery of questions on restrictive trade policies.

The difference in our ability to get supporters and opponents of term limits to alter their previous positions is revealing and is probably at- tributable to the original (that is, precontrary arguments) strength of those positions. Only 13 percent of those favoring term limits said their support was not very strong, whereas 63 percent of those opposing term limits said their opposition was not very strong. Apparently those sup- porting term limits have come to more of a public judgment than those who oppose this reform. So in this sense, opponents of term limits are left with a triple whammy. Not only are their fellow travelers fewer in number, but as a group they are less strong in their convictions and as a result, they are more likely to change their minds when confronted with opposing arguments.

This returns us to a point made earlier. Additional information should not be counted on to save Congress or even, in this case, to derail the movement to reform it. First, much of the misinformation currently works in favor of those wanting to weaken the reform movement. The public does not realize how many staffers members have, how much money members make, or how long members have served, yet it still wants to cut staffs, salaries, and careers. In many cases, the public has not thought through the arguments and counterarguments for reform proposals; but if our brief experiment is any indication, we should not assume that once these arguments are presented and considered the pub- lic will decide that current congressional arrangements are really a good deal. Our results suggest that additional information on the pros and cons of term limits and on the actual levels of staff support, salary, and tenure is likely to make people more desirous of reform. It is easier to talk people out of opposition to term limits than it is to talk them out of support for term limits. For Congress, it is hardly the case that to be known is to be known favorably.

CONCLUSION

It would take a calculator to keep track of all the things people dislike about Congress, but some organization can be imposed on the litany by bearing in mind a few pieces of information about the public's desires and perceptions. People perceive a Washington system that is hard at work sullying the virtuous governmental structures and relationships created in the constitutional system. Congress, owing partly to member missteps, to an eager press, and to its open, collegial structure, is most closely associated in the public mind with this Washington system of special interests and undeserved privileges.

A small portion of Congress's public-relations problems could be solved by providing the public with more accurate information. For example, some people have come to believe that members of Congress are granted certain perquisites that they do not in fact possess. But our results also reveal that the public's misinformation sometimes works to the advantage of Congress. If people really knew the level of staff support, members' salaries, and members' typical length of service, they would be more negative toward Congress than they already are. From what we have learned, the people would not like Congress even if they were fully informed about its features.

A large portion of Congress's public-relations difficulties would vanish if societal problems were magically solved – by anyone or anything – but we take this to be a less than achievable hope. Instead, congressional reform holds the greater and more realistic promise for improving the public's image of Congress. As other surveys have indicated, the public is strongly supportive of a balanced-budget amendment as well as a pay cut and term limits for members. Moreover, support for term limits increases the more people consider the idea and appears to be more than a knee-jerk expression of dissatisfaction. But, unlike wishing for a better-informed public, costs may be associated with certain reforms in terms of Congress's ability to operate. As a result, the possibility exists that enactment of reforms might not lead to greater support for Congress after all. We just do not know.

It is our conclusion that the best strategy for improving the public's views of Congress is two pronged. First, in light of the public's deep-seated belief that Congress has become a creature of the Washington scene, ways must be found to limit the influence of key actors in that scene. Possible reforms of this nature include serious campaign-finance legislation, a continued reduction in perquisites, and further limitations on interest-group activities. We must be more open to proposals of this ilk, remembering that whether or not each reform would "make Congress better" is only part of the issue. An equally important part is whether or not each reform would improve Congress in the eyes of the people. There are ways to make Congress seem less of a mainstay in the evil Washington scene. Any opportunity to do so should be considered seriously.

Still, the people cannot be allowed free rein to alter any and all features of the government's institutional design, because the resultant government would not be based on democratic processes. While Congress can be made to seem a little less attached to the Washington scene, citizens must be made to realize that a major part of their distaste for Congress is endemic to an open legislative body in a large and complicated modern democratic polity. When the issues are complex and far-reaching, and when interests are diverse and specialized, the democratic process will be characterized by disagreements and a pace that can charitably be described as deliberate. And these disagreements will likely be played out by surrogates rather than by ordinary people.

The public performs no useful purpose by adopting the attitude that these surrogates, whether they be members of Congress, leaders of the parties, or officials of interest groups, have messed everything up and all would be right if they would only listen to ordinary people again. The truth is that ordinary people disagree fundamentally on vital issues. The noise and acrimony we despise so much in politics is a reflection of our own diversity and occasional convictions. Democratic procedures are based on Crick's "open canvass of competing interests," and people are put off by this open canvass. People want a level of efficiency that is impossible with open democratic procedures, and they want a level of equity that is unattainable if we accept the public's apparently unshakable assumption that special interests are divorced from public interests.

The kind of information people need to be given is not how many staffers members are provided and whether or not members are allowed a limousine; that would be easy. The people need to be educated on the nature of democratic procedures. They need to be told that these procedures feature public disagreements, debates, compromises, competing interests, conflicting information, and slowness. Our political institutions are paying a price for the fact that people demand democratic procedures and then recoil when exposed to them. Congress pays the biggest price for this situation because it is in Congress that democratic procedures are consistently, nay relentlessly, on display.

Congress is far from blameless. Its members have made missteps, have been too unwilling to consider reforms, and have sometimes even led the chorus of Congress bashers. But Congress should not be blamed for serving as a constant reminder to the people that we have a democratic system of government, with all the messy democratic procedures that come along with it. If people could be made to appreciate deeply the necessity of democratic procedures, support for Congress and for the other political institutions would go up, and a more realistic discussion of how procedures could be improved would be possible.

With descriptions of the basic contours of public perceptions, attitudes, and desires now in place, it is time to recognize the detail and variations existing in public opinion on the topic. To this point, we have made terse, general, and, therefore, somewhat misleading statements about how "the public" feels. In the next chapter, we try to convey some of the nuances of public sentiments by turning to the focus-group sessions. We examine in depth people's attitudes toward the various parts of government and how these attitudes fit together as a coherent whole.

5

Focus groups and perceptions of the Washington system

People want their political institutions and politicians to be efficient and equitable. They believe the Constitution set up a system that meets these demands, but they also believe politics as usual in the late twentieth century is mired in gridlock, the influence of special interests, and neglect of the American public. How do people's evaluations of the constitutional structure and politics as usual in Washington fit together in their minds? How do attitudes about the constitutional system and the Washington system color more specific evaluations of institutions and members? In this chapter we provide a model of how people envision the national government. We investigate in depth the public's thoughts about the two political systems (constitutional and Washington) and how attitudes toward different institutions and members fit together to help people make sense of politics.

To accomplish this task, we must move beyond our dependence on survey data and turn instead to our focus groups. A complete, holistic portrait of attitudes is impossible to elicit over the phone in thirty minutes, no matter how large the sample. The depth and richness of the public mood concerning the two political systems have the potential to be discerned only if people are allowed to expand on their thoughts beyond the constrained time frame and closed-ended questions characteristic of modern telephone polling procedures, and only if they are able to interact with fellow citizens in a setting more typical for the expression of these thoughts than an out-of-the-blue phone conversation with a stranger.

FOCUS GROUPS AS A RESEARCH STRATEGY

Asking people for whom they intend to vote is different from asking about their reflections on political institutions. The former lends itself easily to surveys; the latter does not. As a result, we conducted the focus-group sessions alluded to earlier and described in detail in the Appendix. To this point, we have used the odd quotation from selected focus-group participants to supplement survey results. In this chapter, we make fuller use of the wealth of information generated by these sessions.

For many years now, focus-group research has been utilized heavily in the area of marketing (see Coe & MacLachlan, 1980; Higgenbotham & Cox, 1979). Bringing together not blatantly atypical individuals in small groups for the purpose of observing and monitoring their reactions to prospective advertising slogans, packaging, and products has proven to be an effective method of gauging likely public reaction. The technique came to the attention of the nation largely due to its use in George Bush's election campaign of 1988. The Bush campaign organized several focus-group sessions to try out possible campaign topics for the race against Michael Dukakis. When the participants consistently reacted emotionally and negatively to information on the Massachusetts furlough program as it existed when Dukakis was governor, the "Willie Horton" issue was made a part of the campaign and, by all accounts, hurt Dukakis's chances of winning the election. The apparent effectiveness of focus groups in this case quickly led to their adoption in many subsequent campaigns as a way to pretest reaction to campaign strategies, slogans, issues, and even hairdos.

But focus groups have not been widely accepted as a legitimate methodology of social-science research. Research using focus groups is beginning to appear in scholarly journals (see Conover, Crewe, & Searing, 1991) and books (Gamson, 1992) but is still exceedingly rare. Reservations abound. These reservations may have been most eloquently expressed by Nelson Polsby (1993a,b). Reacting to the Kettering Foundation's use of focus groups to arrive at its conclusion (summarized in Chapter 1) that the political system had "spun out of [popular] control," was "run by a professional political class," and had its "doors closed to the average citizen," Polsby questions the ability of focus-group results to support such conclusions. "A really skilled moderator ought to be able in two short hours to get a focus group of 'approximately 12 people' to say nearly anything" (1993a: 84). Polsby believes that the insights suggested by the focus-group sessions should have been validated by traditional methods before being accepted. He adds that "it would be a pity if influential people thought that what those focus groups allegedly concluded was true in case it isn't true" (1993a: 85).

Polsby's critique elicited a spirited response from the Kettering Foundation. Michael Briand (1993) cites the ability of focus-group research "to get at the concerns, needs, and feelings that underlie people's opinions and preferences" (542). He also is impressed with the potential of focus groups to go beyond survey research, saying, "Even the best scholarly surveys only aggregate opinion – they merely sum individual views. . . . There just is no genuinely public view until the individual members of the public have thought and talked together about what they, as a public, believe, feel, and want" (543).

In light of the controversial nature of focus-group research, we feel compelled to spend a page or two explaining our view of what the approach can and cannot do. Polsby is quite right about the potential for abuse of focus-group research. Of course, this potential is present with survey research as well, as Briand points out. But concerns with the potential bias of survey question wording, question order, and interviewer actions and statements can be minimized by disseminating as much information as possible on these vital matters. It is much more difficult to provide all the relevant information on focus groups. Each session is different. Even the most detailed protocol would not allow subsequent researchers to duplicate procedures as closely as would be possible, at least in theory, with survey research. Replicability is essential to the scientific process, and it is a problem with focus-group research.

But even as we recognize the limitations of focus-group research we must recognize the possibilities. In drafting questions for our national survey, we felt constrained in the kinds of topics we could discuss, in the background information we could provide, and in the depth of responses we could elicit. Surveys facilitate replication, but the ability to replicate is not the only criterion for constructing an appropriate research design. The replication of superficiality is not necessarily a good thing, and a sole reliance on survey research to measure public attitudes toward political institutions would produce nothing more than a superficial understanding of those attitudes.

Thus, we unashamedly utilize focus-group research, but we do so in a way that we believe minimizes the reservations Polsby ably communicates on behalf, we suspect, of many traditional social-science researchers. First, we are obviously utilizing focus-group research in combination with traditional survey research. This combination is a happy one. The two approaches have such different strengths and weaknesses, it only makes sense to include both. The inability to ground focus-group research in vital aspects of the scientific method makes it sensible to use surveys and focus groups in a complementary fashion. This is not an either/or situation. We like the independent verification possible with two widely differing approaches to the problem, and we like combining the rigor of surveys with the depth of the focus groups. We are doubly pleased that independent verification actually occurs in this case. The conclusions we offer are consistent with both the transcripts of the focus groups and the survey results.

Another key factor in our utilization of focus groups is that at the beginning of the research we were not aware of the precise theoretical direction our presentation would take. Some readers may see this as a curious attempt to make a virtue out of theoretical vacuity. Nonetheless, since Polsby is correct about the ability of the focus-group leader to get people to say "nearly anything," it is important to note that we had no idea what we wanted them to say. We knew we wanted to hear what people thought about political institutions and different parts of those institutions, but the moderator had no particular desire to induce damning, Congress-bashing statements or, for that matter, patriotic, our-political-system-is-the-best-in-the-world protestations. Careful review of the written transcripts or audio tapes of the focus-group sessions[1] supports the fact that the moderator of our groups followed a minimalist strategy, trying to keep the herd in the pasture but providing as little other guidance as possible.

The combination of national survey results and focus-group results yields an incredibly valuable collection of information, and we will continue to report a mixture of both types of results. We now turn exclusively to the focus groups, allowing people to state in their own words their perceptions of and attitudes toward political institutions and politicians. Much of what was said in these groups is perfectly consistent with the results of the survey, which substantially boosts confidence in our overall conclusions. But these comments go well beyond anything that could have been gleaned from the survey to provide an intriguing look at public perceptions.

THE TWO POLITICAL SYSTEMS

A beginning premise of our research is that previous work erred in attempting to determine people's overall attitudes toward the political system. We suspected that people would react differently to different parts of the political system – and they do. In fact, evidence from the survey data suggests that people actually see two quite different political systems. The constitutional system, of which the institutions are a part, elicits positive feelings from the public. The Washington system, on the other hand, is evil and nasty, and members of Congress are deeply embedded in it.

Our understanding of the two political systems can only progress so far using survey data. We therefore turned to the focus-group discussions to develop a model of the public's vision of the political systems, displayed in Figure 5.1. The model evolved from our analysis of the focus-

---

1 Transcripts of the focus-group sessions are available from the authors.

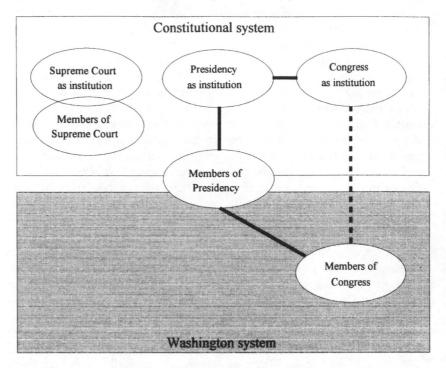

Figure 5.1. The two political systems

group sessions and is intended to be a heuristic device rather than a causal model. That is, Figure 5.1 offers a conceptualization of the general connections commonly made in the public mind among the various parts of the national government. As has become our practice, we separate the purely institutional aspect of the three governmental branches from their membership aspects. We also separate the constitutional system and the Washington system. A solid line indicates a strong linkage in people's minds between two objects, whereas a dotted line indicates a weak linkage. We offer evidence from the focus-group discussions to support this conceptualization throughout the rest of the chapter, but several features of the figure require explication before we turn to the evidence.

First, the focus-group participants did not think frequently about the Supreme Court. When participants were asked to evaluate the government, we specifically mentioned the Supreme Court, the presidency, and Congress, but they rarely responded by talking about the Supreme Court. When they did, the discussion focused more on the Supreme

Court's place in the governmental structure than on the justices, either individually or as a group. Indeed, almost no one mentioned the justices by name or evaluated the Supreme Court in terms of factions on the Court or ideological splits among justices. Hence, in Figure 5.1, "members" of the Supreme Court are intimately connected to the institution since people rarely make a distinction between the two. The public does see the Court immersed in the constitutional system, but the Court is not seen as being strongly tied to other parts of government. It certainly is not viewed as being associated with the Washington system, which is part of the reason for its relatively high levels of support. Thus, no further links are included, and the Court is left a somewhat isolated component of the polity.

Unlike the Supreme Court, when the presidency is viewed by ordinary people, it is necessary to distinguish between the institution of the presidency and the current president. The institution of the presidency is firmly embedded in the constitutional system, though approval of the institution is to some extent related to approval of the current president, and vice versa. When people talk about the presidency, they easily slip into talking about the president (then President Bush). The current president is even seen to some extent as a part of the constitutional system; a mild halo effect is occasionally observable due to the president's prominent place in the institution of the presidency. Most important, neither the current president nor the institution of the presidency is seen by the people as being hopelessly stuck in the mire of the Washington system, though occasionally individual presidents are thought to have mud on their shoes.

The institution of the presidency is strongly linked in people's minds with that of Congress. People often discussed the presidency as an institution in relational terms with the Congress. Separation of powers and checks and balances are part of people's attitude structures concerning these two institutions.

Finally, evaluations of the sitting president are related to evaluations of the congressional membership. Discussions of President Bush were strongly connected to discussions of the members of Congress. Both fit under the general umbrella of "politician" and both were often assessed in terms of the upcoming election. Concerns about the gridlock between Bush and the Congress were often mentioned. It is important that gridlock was seen as a product of the people in office and not of the constitutional system.

The institution of Congress is embedded in the constitutional system, just as are the other two institutions, and accrues benefits simply by being part of this system. But the institution of Congress is only weakly tied to the current membership of Congress, which means that the members do not benefit from much of a halo effect. Where does this leave the members of Congress?

The most glaring feature of the figure is the public's unequivocal placement of the membership of Congress in the Washington system. Years ago, Morris Fiorina wrote about Congress being a "keystone to the Washington establishment" (1977) due to its ability to shape other parts of the government to meet its own needs. Be that as it may, the public certainly believes Congress is a keystone of the Washington system, interacting daily with the power brokers, special interests, parties, fundraisers, and perquisites. This connection of the members of Congress with the Washington system explains the breadth and depth of public disgruntlement with congressional membership, particularly when we add the fact that Congress is viewed as being so powerful relative to the other institutions. The public believes that members of Congress are lazy, scandal-plagued, pampered, self-serving, and out of touch. The Washington system has made them so. One's own representative might be struggling against these forces and, if so, invariably loses. People therefore perceive the membership as being distant, inaccessible, and inattentive.

THE PEOPLE'S LANGUAGE

This model was derived from ordinary people talking about politics. The way people talk about their government provides important insights into both the hopes they have for the political system and the way they organize and process information about it. In this section, we explore, in order, participants' attitudes toward national political institutions, toward the people in them, and toward the responsibilities of citizens. When all these disparate thoughts and feelings are considered as a coherent whole, the result is a startling picture of how citizens view the political system – or, more accurately, the political *systems*.

Institutional relationships and power

When discussing national institutions, many of the focus-group participants seemed relatively well versed on how the institutions were set up and on the constitutional roles they were meant to play. Indeed, in almost all of the eight focus groups, at least one person provided a short civics lesson on the powers of the presidency, the Supreme Court, and the Congress. For example, Barb from New York said:

Perceptions of the Washington system

Congress is the most powerful element because they make the laws. The Supreme Court rules on the laws. The president has a certain amount of power, but frankly other than the military and his veto power, what actual power does the president of the United States have?

Sally from Nebraska focused on the relationship between Congress and the presidency:

Between the Congress you've got the two houses, you've got the one that's divided according to population and the other one gives each state equal representation. But the two houses sort of balance with each other and have to come to some sort of an agreement before they can even get a law passed. And then if the President doesn't agree with it he can veto it. Well, the only thing that can override that . . . I think it's a two-thirds vote that it takes to override the veto. And they can't always drum that up.

Maybe all those students in American Politics 101 were not sleeping through lectures after all. Regardless, this civics-text emphasis in discussions of the institutions usually reflected an understanding of and fondness for the larger constitutional design. Not surprisingly, participants strongly believed that this constitutional structure is the best structure possible.

Yet many participants felt that the original design is endangered by the possibility of one institution gaining inordinate power over the other two. We asked focus-group participants which branch of government they thought was the most powerful and received each of the three possible answers. A few people said that the Supreme Court was the most powerful because it "has the last say on things," "the president doesn't have power over the Supreme Court," and "it makes decisions that everyone has to live by, including Congress and senators and so forth." These people, however, were in the minority. In fact, most participants indicated that the Supreme Court was a minor player and went for the most part unnoticed. The following comments were typical:

It seems like Congress gets more of the attention, they're passing this and they're passing that, but it really seems like the Supreme Court is out of the picture. (Nebraska)

Joe: The Supreme Court, you know, they get appointed to that for life. I don't think that's right. . . . But to me the Supreme Court doesn't really, I don't think they do a whole lot for the people.
Bill: I think they respond more to challenges of the law than they actually write in laws or set any kind of new precedents. (Texas)

Actually, if things are run right the Supreme Court wouldn't have anything to do. Really, I mean if everything is run the way it's supposed to, all the problems and everything runs according to the Constitution, they should be a bunch of old men having a good time. (New York)

The Supreme Court may hold a hallowed place in the institutional structure, but most people do not perceive it as playing a major role in the day-to-day decisions of the political system. Thus, when they think of the Supreme Court, they are more likely to envision its constitutional role than its day-to-day contributions to governing. This is all to the good as far as public support for the Court is concerned.[2]

Focus-group participants disagreed more strongly about the extent to which the presidency is powerful. Some people thought the presidency was the most powerful of the three, but a larger number of focus-group participants argued that the presidency was by far the weakest branch, having little or no power in the political system. As noted in Chapter 3, it was eerily common for people to compare the presidency in the U.S. to the monarchy in Great Britain.

We think of [the president] as like a figurehead. You know, if he's in there supposedly the American people all voted for him, the majority. And so maybe we figure that he's like a figurehead, maybe sort of like the king or queen would be in England. (New York)

Well, the presidency I think is kind of a figurehead position limited in power by the Congress. (Minnesota)

I think of the president as mostly just a figurehead. . . . Well, he's symbolic. (Texas)

Most often, the comments directed at the weakness of the presidency were nestled in comparisons with the power of Congress. The presidency should be the most powerful branch, according to some participants, but in reality Congress has all of the power and uses it to keep the president from getting anything done.

John: I think the president needs to have more power. We elect a president and then if he says something and the Congress comes in and says "No, you can't do that," what did we get this guy for, you know? What did we vote him in for if he can't be the one that takes control?
Margaret: He should have the final word. (Texas)

Well, the presidency, I think, is kind of a figurehead position limited in power by the Congress. And no matter how much you like an individual, now he can probably put a little bit of pressure on, but it's owned and regulated and operated by our Congress. (Minnesota)

2 The one exception, as might be expected, is the abortion issue. A few people in the focus groups raised abortion as an issue the government should be doing something about, and some people blamed the Supreme Court for making the issue more contentious than they thought it should be.

Frequently, the focus-group participants took sides and argued in support of the presidency or Congress. A good example of such an exchange took place in one of the Nebraska focus groups.

Lois: I still think that the president is the most powerful, because the president has the veto power. And there are laws that Congress wants to pass but they got vetoed every time and they can't override them. So I think that at least where it's the bills that don't get overridden the president has the power, that has the most power.

Dan: But they could still do the veto with the two-thirds vote.

Lois: Yeah, but on so many issues they haven't done it.

Dan: Which is what he's doing with the veto. . . . All he's doing is saying, "Fine, you don't do what I want to do? Fine, we'll throw it back at you and you can play with it for two more years. Two more years after and you won't be in office."

Lois: But what I'm saying is that he vetoes it and sends it back to the House and the Senate and they can't override it and so therefore his power is greater than theirs.

Dan: Excuse me, the Congress has already taken away from him the power to declare war, the president can't.

Lois: But he can loophole that – therefore he's more powerful than the Congress.

Maybe a few people *were* sleeping in those 101 lectures, but the main point is that most focus-group participants firmly believed that Congress is the most powerful branch, just as half of the survey respondents thought Congress had too much power (see Chapter 3). For example, Bill from Texas said, "Congress has got a lot more power than the president – they do a lot more. Good, bad or otherwise, they do a lot more." With this perceived power comes attributed responsibility when things go wrong. Many focus-group participants blamed Congress for what they saw as a mess in government.

The Congress are the ones that the president and everybody else has to go to to get them to approve things. They got to vote on it, and they're torn between themselves. So the whole works is messed up right there. That's what causes all the problems. (Texas)

The focus-group participants expressed a willingness either to hold the president and Congress jointly responsible for national problems, including problems with the economy, or, more likely, to turn their full blame on Congress since it is seen as the single most powerful actor in the political system. The survey respondents, as we have seen, showed a similar willingness to hold Congress responsible for not dealing with the most important problem facing the nation, as they saw it, or with the budget deficit. We are quite confident of this finding; yet this perceived power of Congress is not usually reflected in previous research, whether on perceptions of institutional power or on the public's attribution of responsibility across governmental units.

People in government

While the focus-group participants were able to talk about the institutions of government in terms of intended constitutional structure and actual perceived power, their discussions of the presidency and Congress quickly and fluidly turned to the individuals who inhabit these institutions. And just what are the public's perceptions of the people in government?

Politicians almost invariably received low marks from the focus-group participants. In fact, statements about politicians in Washington reflected a highly alienated, disaffected public attitude. A few participants made sweeping statements that all politicians are liars. In New York, two participants summarized a lengthy discussion about politicians this way:

Dolores: The trouble is too many people in the government have lied to the American people too many times, and it's coming home to roost.
Sue: We're finding out that we had faith in them, and we thought they were honest with us, but they're not.

Focus-group participants also complained that politicians spend too much time worrying about reelection, saying one thing during the election campaign and then doing another once in office. They were also concerned that politicians seem to hold a double standard: "[Politicians say,] 'Do as I say, not as I do.' It's like the rules apply to everybody else except them" (Texas). Focus-group participants were obviously highly dissatisfied with politicians in general and quickly drew upon their "politician" stereotype – politicians are dishonest and self-centered.

In what ways are politicians failing? The participants emphasized three areas. First, a number of people argued that politicians need to start listening to the public because they have lost touch with what the people want and need. If they would listen, they could begin to take care of the problems at home. Second, participants emphasized that politicians simply need to do something to take care of society's problems at home. One participant said that she did not know what to do to remedy the problems, but that politicians are supposed to know the answers and should therefore take some action. Many participants seemed to believe that politicians were simply sitting around in Washington not doing any work. If government officials would work, then maybe the problems facing the United States would disappear. Finally, a few participants stated that they wanted politicians to admit their mistakes rather than constantly try to cover them up.

I'd love to hear somebody say for a change, "Yep, I screwed up. I mean, yeah, I did support this, and that was wrong . . . and I blew it," instead of saying, "I can't remember that." If I could just hear somebody say, "I really screwed up on that, and I learned my lesson, and I won't do it again." (Minnesota)

Supreme Court justices. Focus-group participants also moved beyond general comments about politicians to make separate remarks about the Supreme Court justices, the president, and members of Congress. Comments on the Supreme Court justices were the most rare. Indeed, in only two instances did participants focus on the justices, and both times the concern was with the life tenure of the justices and the nomination process that leads to their appointment. For example:

Dan: Put somebody on the Supreme Court that's only forty years old and the guy's got a locked-up job for the next fifty years at a 100-plus thousand a year or whatever it is.
   Lois: Because they aren't appointed by us, we don't really have any say in what they do . . . and the people who are there now were appointed years ago in different administrations so they are not even controlled by the voters. (Nebraska)

Comments on the Supreme Court justices, however, were highly unusual. Most participants, when they talked about the Court at all, focused on its institutional aspect, not on the people who constitute it.

The president. Discussions of the president (George Bush at the time the focus groups were conducted) and of the candidates running for president were much more common. Most comments about President Bush were critical and highlighted three perceived problems. First, people argued that Bush was paying too much attention to problems in foreign countries and not enough to problems at home: "[Bush] has taken care of everybody out in the other countries, but home has more or less fallen apart while he's been doing this" (New York). Second, several people were upset that Bush would not admit, or did not see, the economic problems facing the nation. These feelings were expressed most frequently in areas of the country hard hit by increased unemployment, such as New York. Finally, some participants complained that Bush had not done anything in four years. As Jack from Texas said, "Look at Bush. He's been in there for four years and he's done nothing. Now he wants to bring more employment, more this and more that. What happened to the four years he was in there? Why didn't he do something then?" At the same time, several people defended Bush's record, making the arguments that he had only had four years to get anything done, that Congress had done everything in its power to stall Bush's domestic program, and even that Bush was still trying to clean up the problems left him by the Reagan administration.

Since the focus groups were conducted during 1992, the discussions often turned to the presidential campaigns. Participants were eager to talk about George Bush, Bill Clinton, and Ross Perot. Specifically, the hottest topics concerned campaign promises, the impact of Perot on the election, the character of the candidates, and the occasional policy proposal. Some participants also raised concerns about divided government: if Bush were reelected, would Congress continue to refuse to work with him? If so, these people argued, perhaps it would be best to have the same party control both the Congress and the presidency.

Members of Congress. While focus-group participants were generally excited about and interested in the presidential campaign, they saved their most affect-laden comments for members of Congress. The participants felt an overwhelming sense of dissatisfaction when it came to members of Congress, and this dissatisfaction centered around several themes.

First, people were upset by the scandals that have plagued Congress, corroborating our survey results discussed in Chapter 4. The 1992 House bank scandal drew the heaviest criticism, in part because it was fresh in their minds and in part because people processed this information in very personal terms. If the participants could keep their own checkbooks balanced, why couldn't members of Congress? The bank scandal was something people could easily relate to because they continuously have to deal with balancing their checkbooks. But participants were not upset simply because some members overdrew their bank accounts. They claimed to be worried about what such behavior meant for the political system.

Mike: You're entrusting them with your lives, your country and all your money; and they're so frivolous about a checking account.
Joan: You know it. I mean, those men that are in there to me are supposed to be really brainy men.
Mike: They were elected. That doesn't mean they were brainy.
Dolores: Well, if they can't handle their own checkbook, it makes you worry about what they're doing with all your tax money. (New York)

Some participants were able to find a positive outcome in the bank scandal: "Well, there's a good side to [the bank scandal] too. I mean, that cleaned out more incumbents than any election you've ever had" (New York).

Participants were also disgruntled about the pay raise members of

Congress voted for themselves. Cindy from Texas said the pay raise was "a direct slap in the face." Sue from New York said she felt impotent when Congress does things like pass a pay raise, that no matter how much "people yell and scream, the pay raise goes through. We have no way to stop it. They want to do something, they do it." People were especially upset with the pay raise in light of the state of the economy at the time.

Second, there was widespread concern that Congress simply was not getting anything done. Similar to the worries expressed about George Bush, participants believed that with the extensive problems facing the nation, Congress should have been doing *something* to eradicate them. One participant in Minnesota argued that even when Congress does do something, the legislation passed often maintains the status quo and does not make real progress. But the most colorful exchanges occurred when participants argued that Congress was simply doing nothing.

In Congress, they got cobwebs on their arms from sitting in chairs for three years. They got no new ideas. They just keep going back to the old stuff that keeps putting money in their pockets. (New York)

Bob: I think that there has to be major communication between . . . the Democrats and Republicans and the Senate and the House, you know, everybody. Just have to say, "There's a problem. We won't leave this room until it's fixed."
Lisa: They never could do that.
Barb: Take them all to Camp David.
Lisa: No, they don't deserve anything that good. They need to be put in small spaces in the summertime that is not air conditioned, and say, "Get on the ball and do something!" and they'd do it. (New York)

Our representatives should be serving us a hell of a lot better than what they are. I really don't know what they've done. (Minnesota)

While participants were cynical about the job members of Congress were doing, a positive note is that people seemed to believe that members of Congress could do the job if they would just put their minds to it. In essence, members were seen as having the ability but not the will to take care of the nation's problems.

The third and most prevalent concern was that members of Congress had lost touch with the public, with constituents, with majority opinion, and with real people. We emphasized in Chapter 4 that survey respondents believed that members of Congress were far removed from ordinary people and had lost touch with the public, a belief held strongly by the focus-group participants. Indeed, this belief that Congress members were inattentive, unresponsive, and out of touch was so widespread that it colored much of the discussion of Congress. Numerous participants made general comments about Congress members losing touch.

97

They just don't pay attention to the issues that really affect people. I don't think they take into account how the rest of the country is being affected. They're too insulated. (Texas)

Molly: I think the vast majority of Congress's members have no idea really what the people's wishes are.
Steve: They are in touch with the extremes. Those are the people that they listen to and they're the ones that pull their strings, right? But the majority doesn't scream and shout. (Nebraska)

When I think about it, [Congress] seems very removed from the people, and yet they're elected officials of the people, of course, but . . . they don't seem accessible to me. (Minnesota)

In the beginning they know what we want and they kind of tell us whatever we want. . . . But then once they get there they forget all that and they don't really seem to even care what you want, or what you put them in there to represent. I don't think they have any idea about what anyone wants. (Texas)

Focus-group participants offered several explanations for why this inattentiveness was so rampant. These explanations provide important clues to the bases of people's attitudes concerning members of Congress. One explanation focused on the class bias in the political system. This view, most frequently offered by participants from Texas, held that class differences between members of Congress and many people in the United States made representation impossible.

Forget about the poor person, the poor person doesn't stand a chance. They're just trying to make ends meet, and they still can't make it. . . . But the people that, as they say, were born with a silver spoon in their mouth, they've got it easy. And this is what the Congress is, they're all these people who were born with a silver spoon in their mouth, where they've got it made. They don't have any problems, any worries. They make it look like they do, but they don't. (Texas)

The wealthy put their own in office. And as long as it's like that, we are not going to get represented. . . . They might go back to their community, but not this community. It's the rich community they go visit. So even if they say they come back, it's to a different community. (Texas)

According to this view, members of Congress are unaware of the needs and wants of the American public because they cannot begin to understand the difficulties confronted by poor people. Since they are wealthy, Congress members cannot, and do not, take care of the problems of the poor.

A second explanation also focused on money, not in terms of class bias but as the means by which members of Congress are drawn away from serving their constituents' interests. Money, according to several people, drives the political system. And who controls the money? Big business and special-interest groups.

The Congressmen are listening to the lobbyists. They are not listening to the people. So for me I feel helpless and hopeless about the Congress, about their listening to people. (New York)

These guys are up there, pardon my language, like fat cats as they've been called, doing this, that, and the other, and they're hobnobbing with who? The people who have the influence, and who has the influence? The people with the money. (Texas)

I think there's too much influence in the Congress on the congressmen by, not the people, but by the special-interest groups and the PACs that put them in office. (Nebraska)

Moderator: What's gone wrong? Why do you think Congress is not responding?
   Jack: Big money has bought 'em out.
   Cindy: Money is more important than people. (Texas)

Money buys anybody out. (Texas)

A major problem with the predominant influence of money is that it makes members of Congress lose touch with the public. According to this view, Congress members pay attention to whomever has the most money. Since the average person does not have money, he or she is ignored.

Why would [a member of Congress] want to come and talk to us this morning? Could we get a pot [of money] together or something? So why would he want to waste his time? But you let a bunch of executives or corporations sit around, he knows there's going to be millions of dollars thrown in his pot, and that's what it amounts to. He don't want to come back and talk to us, all we're going to do is give him a lot of headache, static. Talk to him and he'll go back with a headache. He don't want that, he avoids us. The only time he'll come around is election time. (Texas)

A third explanation focused on the idea that the perquisites members of Congress receive once in office make them lose touch with the average person. Once they live the good life in Washington, they forget how average people have it and therefore become inattentive to their needs. The Washington system co-opts them (see Chapter 4).

I think Congress . . . has gotten too big for their britches. They got used to all the freebies, the perks, the nice things that come to them, the power, and it's just become taken for granted. It's become abused. (Nebraska)

I think they should mandate a rule that any elected member of government should spend a certain amount of time not sitting in his ivory tower. They ought to make this guy get out in a regular car, with or without air conditioning, with or without a chauffeur, certainly no stretch limo, and make him drive around the neighborhood that elected him and the neighborhoods that didn't. (Texas)

A number of focus-group participants commented that members of Congress should be forced to return to their community frequently to see how people really live. One person even suggested that, by law, members of Congress should be limited to six months in Washington and should be required to spend the other six months in their districts.

A question naturally arising from these various explanations of members' failings is whether voters believe they are simply electing the wrong people to office or whether they believe the system ruins good people. More than half of the survey respondents said Congress ruins good people, and another quarter felt that it is a combination of bad people and a corrupting system (see Chapter 4). The focus-group participants also came down rather firmly on the system, saying that people who are elected to office are generally good, but once they get to Washington they become corrupted.

They had good ideas and lofty ideals, but somewhere along the way they've been corrupted. (New York)

You find so many good people going in and the next thing you know they're corrupted. (Texas)

The people that voted for him, we voted for him based on what he told us in the beginning. Now he may feel that way or he may not. You're choosing to believe that that's the way he felt. Six months, two years, three years down the road you don't know what that guy really believes in . . . because of the corruption that he's dealt with in Washington. (Texas)

I think maybe some of them might have good intentions, but when they get in there it's like a corrupt system. They have to start going alone against the whole works, you know. (Texas)

You're trying to please everybody, and somehow you pretty much can end up losing your integrity by doing that, and you have to keep backing up saying, "OK now, what's really important here?" and that's hard to do when you're bombarded with all this stuff that says you need to do this and you need to do this . . . and you can't do it all. (Minnesota)

Washington – the perks, the game of politics, and the money floating around – corrupts even good people. The feelings of impotence and despair produced by this view are strong. When people think about members of Congress, therefore, their attitudes about the membership are firmly linked to beliefs about the corrupt Washington system. This linkage feeds into the negative evaluations of the members of Congress: even if they are good to begin with, they will quickly become bad.

Perceptions of the Washington system

Citizen responsibilities and actions

The focus-group participants were clearly frustrated with the people in government, especially the members of Congress. Much of the blame for problems in the system, according to these people, falls on members of Congress who are simply not doing the job they were put in office to do. But assessments of responsibility are significantly more complex than this picture implies. Participants *do* blame the people in government, but they also are quite willing to blame themselves. We were surprised at the extent to which participants directed much blame not only at citizens in general, but also at themselves in particular.

A few people were disillusioned with politics to the point of being alienated from the political system. The frustrations they experienced when dealing with and observing politics led them to conclude that their input makes no difference.

People are at the point now where they are disillusioned. It's like, "Why bother?" (New York)

I think everybody just feels kind of overwhelmed, and they're just throwing their hands in the air, and say "What comes, comes." (New York)

It's just really frustrating. What difference does [voting] make if we get the same idiots over and over again? (Nebraska)

I don't think it's a case of the people feeling like they don't care. I think they do care. I think that they've gotten to such a level of frustration that they feel, "What difference does my vote make?" (Texas)

If participating in politics simply perpetuates the dysfunctions currently plaguing the nation, then why get involved?

Yet this view was expressed by a surprisingly small number of people. Most of the participants argued that citizen input can make a difference and that citizens need to do more, that they need to take the initiative if the U.S. government is to be improved. What do citizens need to do? People emphasized the need to be better informed and to vote regularly.

We have a great power. We have the power of the vote. If we don't like that yutz that's doing his thing in Washington, DC, he's not going to be there long, not if enough people get irritated at him and say, "You're not doing a thing for me. Go away!" (Nebraska)

We need to become more informed about what the issues are and what we agree with and what we don't agree with, so that we can form a more intelligent opinion about who's running and who we should vote for. And get out there and vote. Because people can sit around and they can bitch all day, but if you don't get out and do something about it, nothing's going to happen. (Nebraska)

As complicated as government is . . . the better informed we are about the overall picture the better off we're all going to be and the better choices we can make. (Texas)

For the political system to work properly, people believe they must take the initiative to learn what is going on in the government, to track the decisions of elected officials, and to obtain as much information as possible about candidates running for office (see also Theiss-Morse, 1993). If citizens are willing to expend the energy to become well informed, then they will be able to vote according to what they want rather than feeling as if they are passive onlookers in an unresponsive political system.

The vast majority of focus-group participants explained their lack of involvement by referring to their busy lives, which leave little if any time for politics.

I think we should become more active, but . . . a lot of times we are just so consumed with having to work. You know, some people have to work two jobs, the mother has to work outside the home to make ends meet, but there usually just isn't any time . . . to get active in your community, and it's right out of necessity I think that we have become so centered in our home. (Nebraska)

Today in families both of the parents have to work in order to get along. So by the time they work, they take care of their family, you know, they've got all they can handle just to get by. I mean . . . they have the feeling "Well, I'm not going to make a difference," and they just get so busy. They're just so busy with life. They just don't have the time. (New York)

Most Americans don't have time in their day to just sit around and read and study politicians to find out what their platform is. It's very difficult. . . . So people say, "The hell with it, I don't have time to vote." (Nebraska)

People realize they should be more active in politics, but they believe they just do not have the time. Still, many focus-group participants saw political involvement as essential to correcting the flaws of the political system, arguing that being too busy does not absolve citizens of their responsibilities.

If we don't get off our duffs and vote, we have nobody to blame but ourselves. (Nebraska)

[Members of Congress are] not doing the job, but we aren't doing our job. I think we've lost interest. We've put other things before our government. (New York)

The most frustrating thing for me in terms of being mad at government, being mad at Congress, blaming Congress, is that less than half of us vote, and even fewer vote in the off presidential years. I mean what right do we have to whine and moan about what's going on if we haven't even said what we want? You know, you haven't gone out and voted about it. (Nebraska)

I think we really have to blame ourselves a lot. We cop out on our need to get involved, and I can say that from personal experience. (Minnesota)

People may be upset with members of Congress, but they are also upset with themselves. Citizens recognize that they are in part responsible for the problems of the political system. In fact, some participants saw lack of citizen involvement as the main source of the problem, pointing out that members of Congress may find their hands tied because citizens do not let them know what they think.

It is easy to blame the people at the top, and I do put a lot of blame on the people up on top for our problems. But I do think it all comes down to individual responsibility and knowing what the issues are. . . . I really think it comes down to being able to look at the big picture and being able to look past yourself and taking responsibility yourself. (Minnesota)

I don't think enough people complain to their Congressmen, you know, that we take that time to complain to them. I don't think [members of Congress] feel we're really interested so they just kind of slide by. (New York)

If we don't demand anything, then why should they do anything? (Texas)

If people fulfilled their duties as citizens, then elected officials, including members of Congress, would have a better idea what people wanted and would act accordingly. As the situation stands now, members of Congress are to a great extent left in the dark since citizens do not take the time to make informed demands. What makes the prevalence of this opinion startling is that it is being voiced not by members of Congress looking for an excuse but by the people themselves.

CONCLUSION

We began this chapter defending our use of focus groups. Focus-group participants could tell us things we did not expect to hear. We could discover deeply held beliefs rather than rely on the potentially superficial opinions gathered from the survey. The focus-group setting allowed for the social interaction common to political discussions. And we could better gauge how people structured their attitudes concerning the political system, thereby determining which attitudes fit together in people's minds.

The actual results from the focus-group analysis prove our defense was well founded. The focus-group participants revealed to us unexpected and deeply held beliefs about the political system that fit together in an understandable way. The results provide a rich, meaningful view of public attitudes toward the institutions and membership of Congress, the Supreme Court, and the presidency. They also clearly corroborate the survey findings discussed in the preceding chapters, thereby increasing confidence in our assessments of the public mood.

Citizens readily admit that they themselves are not blameless. Indeed, the focus-group participants quickly pointed to the unmet responsibilities of citizens to participate actively, to become well informed, and to let members of Congress know what they do and do not want. A big part of the problem with the U.S. government, they believe, is that citizens are not fulfilling these basic responsibilities of democratic citizenship.

This point is crucial because it adds an important twist to the findings of earlier focus-group research, specifically the Kettering Foundation Report. Our results support those of the Kettering Foundation in that participants definitely believe the political system is now out of their control. They believe it is run by a "powerful professional political class" and that "votes no longer make much difference because money rules" (Matthews, 1991: 78). To that point, Kettering is right on the money.

But the Kettering Report is also filled with references to how the people are anxious to participate, but the naughty system will not let them. It turns out that the people are much more willing to shoulder some of the blame themselves than the Kettering Foundation is to distribute any blame to the people. People believe problems exist and that some of them are due to their own inability or unwillingness to engage in politics. Whereas Kettering believes that the people have been forced to disengage, the people themselves admit that part of the disengagement was voluntary, owing to demanding schedules, sloth, and disinterest.

Moreover, it is unfortunate that Kettering and so much other previous research was less than careful in distinguishing among specific referents. Blanket questions about how the public feels toward some generic "system" simply confuse the issue. A complex system entails so many components, features, institutions, and subsystems that a more focused approach is essential. When such an approach is provided we see that people's indictment of the political system is not nearly as unequivocal as might be imagined. They like parts of the system: they like the Constitution; they like the institutions of Congress, the presidency, and the Supreme Court; and they often like their own member of Congress.

Indeed, anything connected with the constitutional system elicits a positive response. In the minds of the people, this constitutional system is goodness and light. The Constitution created three political institutions and arranged them in an ingeniously balanced fashion. To the extent there are problems with the political system it is because we have deviated from what was outlined in the Constitution, not because that outline was flawed.

And deviated we have, especially when it comes to members of Congress. We argue that the major reason for this dissatisfaction is that the membership is connected in the public mind with the Washington system. This Washington system is, we believe, what the Kettering Report confuses with the overall political system. The people believe the Washington system is base and invidious, evil incarnate, and runs on greed and special privilege. The greed of politicians makes them susceptible to special interests and they then respond to those interests. The result is that the politicians and special interests find themselves with a cornucopia of undeserved benefits, whereas citizens are left with a few scraps.

The two systems live in a parasitic relationship, the Washington system feeding off of and weakening the constitutional system. Public opinion of other entities within the overall political system, not surprisingly, is influenced by how they are perceived relative to these two systems. The more something is connected in the public mind with the constitutional system, the better off it will be; the more it is connected with the Washington system, the greater the public's dislike for it.

While we believe that part of the reason for the public's aversion to this Washington system is well-placed and that this system could be cleaned up and improved with thoughtful reforms and with a sensitivity to the importance of public perceptions, we also believe that part of the aversion to this Washington system can be traced to the public's disdain for modern democratic processes. These processes are bound to include some aspects of professionalized government, representatives of certain societal interests, and a pace that might make it appear that politicians are doing nothing.

We are not at all inclined to defend the Washington system, particularly the public's vision of it. Important steps need to be taken to reassure people that monied interests are not getting preferential treatment, that politicians are not receiving unnecessary perquisites, and that special interests are sometimes our interests. At the same time, the public occasionally expresses a lack of understanding of what comes with modern democracy and democratic procedures. This lack of understanding was very apparent in the focus groups and confirms our earlier statements concerning a reason behind public disgruntlement with Congress: when viewing the modern Congress, people see clearly the democratic procedures they sometimes claim to like but, in actuality, do not like in the least.

But it is now time to move beyond general discussions of public opinion to an analysis of variations in support for Congress. We use this analysis of variations to learn more about the nature of the relationship between the people and their political institutions. What kind of people are more or less supportive of Congress? What variables seem to be the most successful at explaining variations in support? These are the questions that now move to center stage.

6

Who approves of Congress?

Conversations among focus-group participants highlight the fact that while disgust with Congress is widespread, people differ in their actual level of support and in the reasons behind their evaluations of Congress. These focus-group results provide important clues to ascertaining why the public mood is so negative, but we need to go one step farther to determine the precise identities of Congress's supporters and detractors. We therefore return to our national survey to examine systematically variations in public approval of Congress, and to explain what about Congress the public dislikes and, occasionally, likes.

CONGRESS EQUALS THE MEMBERS OF CONGRESS

Who approves of Congress depends upon what is meant by "Congress." As we have stressed repeatedly, Congress can be seen as a collection of 535 individuals or as a political institution that is quite detached from such ephemeral features as the current membership composition. We now know that only 24 percent of the population approve of Congress the collection of members, whereas 88 percent approve of Congress the permanent institution. But this tremendous difference in mean approval says nothing of the kinds of people who are more likely to approve or disapprove. Just who are the unusual creatures who actually approve of the membership of Congress? Who are the even more unusual creatures who disapprove of the institution of Congress? Do the same traits explain variation in support for the members and for the institution?

We shall answer these questions shortly, but first we must address an intriguing question that helps to clarify our argument. How can 88 percent of the people approve of the institution of Congress, when media polls routinely show that the public vehemently disapproves of Congress? Perhaps either our results or the results of typical media polls are incorrect. Actually, the solution to the puzzle is simple and involves no procedural errors on either side.

We contend that when people are asked what they think of Congress, with no additional specifications provided in the question (as is usually the case with such questions), the answer given is very much an evaluation of the membership of Congress, not of the institution. People think about Congress in terms of its members primarily because their exposure to Congress usually comes through the actions of the membership. When people are specifically asked to evaluate Congress the institution, this evaluation does not come naturally. They must be coaxed to think about the institution. In this sense, people's strong approval of Congress as an institution is seldom a factor in the day-to-day evaluations about which we hear so much. Support for Congress as an institution is there but it is deep and not easily called to mind.

Evidence that supports our interpretation is readily available in the national survey we conducted. In addition to asking respondents whether they approved of the membership of Congress and the institution of Congress, we also obtained a measure of their overall evaluation of Congress with no mention of either member or institutional components. At the beginning of the survey, respondents were given an opportunity to comment on what they liked and disliked about Congress, however they perceived it. Comparing the number of positive and negative remarks of each person gives a sense of their feelings toward Congress, period. Questions referring specifically to the members or the institution came later. These three separate evaluations, one of Congress, one of its members, and one of the institution, were then correlated with a fairly standard battery of demographic and political variables (see Appendix).

Table 6.1 presents the simple bivariate correlations between these variables and the three different evaluations of Congress. The point we wish to make with this table is that the pattern of relationships for approval of the membership of Congress is nearly identical to the pattern of relationships for approval of Congress generally. The signs for the two sets of coefficients are identical for all seven variables and, with the sole exception of external efficacy, so is the pattern of achieving statistical significance.

Contrast these similarities with the differences apparent when the comparison shifts to evaluations of Congress the institution and evaluations of Congress generally. In four of the seven cases, the signs are in opposite directions (and in two of the four both correlations are significant). Efficacy, ideology, and party identification are in the same direction, but never do both correlations achieve significance. The bottom

Table 6.1. *Bivariate correlations of demographic and attitudinal variables with referents of Congress*

Variables	"Generic" Congress	Members of Congress	Congress as Institution
Sex	-.06*	-.10**	.03
Education	-.003	-.04	.18**
Income	-.06*	-.14**	.15**
Party identification	-.08**	-.21**	-.004
Ideology	-.10**	-.14**	-.04
External efficacy	.05	.22**	.18**
Political involvement	-.15**	-.11**	.18**

Note: * *p* < .05; ** *p* < .01

line is that when people are asked to evaluate Congress without further specification, their evaluations seem to be based on the same factors as their evaluations of the membership of Congress, and are very different from the evaluations of the institution of Congress.

As has been the case for much of our research, the focus groups mesh nicely with the survey results. Focus-group participants seemed often to use the phrase "Congress are . . . ." This apparent disagreement between subject and verb may not be an actual disagreement if Congress is seen as plural. Many people see Congress this way, not because it is two houses but because it is 535 members. Thus, when people evaluate Congress they are evaluating its members. An appreciation of this point is crucial for understanding the public's lack of approval of Congress.

BIVARIATE RELATIONSHIPS

The relationship of these seven variables with evaluations of Congress deserves more attention. How well does knowing a person's gender, party affiliation, ideology, income level, educational level, sense of political efficacy, and political involvement allow us to predict that same person's level of approval of Congress? We examine each of these seven variables individually, albeit briefly. We focus on the relationship between these seven variables and evaluations of the congressional membership, since we now know that most people see Congress as equivalent to its members.

Conventional wisdom would lead us to expect that educated, well-off, liberal, Democratic, politically efficacious, and involved males would be more approving of Congress. After all, prior to 1995, congressional membership in recent decades has been predominantly male and Democratic. Moreover, people who are educated, efficacious, involved, and financially well-off are more likely to be comfortable with current political structures. The bivariate results, however, are occasionally surprising and are presented in Figure 6.1.

Perhaps the place to begin is to note that no group is particularly fond of Congress. Sixty-four percent of even the most supportive single group (Democrats) disapprove of Congress. Still, some groups are less disapproving than others. Women, for example, are more likely to approve of Congress than men, 28 percent to 20 percent, despite the fact that there are so few women in Congress; indeed, there were even fewer in 1992 when the survey was conducted.

Some people's higher approval levels are not surprising. Feelings of efficacy behave predictably in that respondents with high levels of external efficacy are more likely to approve of Congress. Party identification and ideology also follow the pattern we would expect given that Democrats had been the majority party in Congress for forty years, until the 1994 elections. Democrats were much more supportive of Congress than were Independents and Republicans, and liberals were more supportive than were moderates or conservatives. Presumably, these patterns reversed with the coming to power of the Republicans in the 104th Congress. So, to some extent, respondents do see Congress through a partisan and/or ideological lens. This is not too surprising in light of our conclusion that Congress is seen as the sum of its members. If these members as a group tend to be of a different partisan or ideological persuasion than the respondent, views of "Congress" will be less charitable.

The remaining three variables – income, education, and political involvement – do not follow expected patterns. The most supportive income group is composed of those making less than $25,000 per year. Similarly, the most supportive educational group consists of those with a high school education or less. Finally, respondents least involved in politics are more approving of Congress than active citizens. These findings concerning education and political involvement are very surprising indeed. Educated and politically involved people should be more supportive of government in general and should better understand and tolerate constraints on legislative behavior. They should therefore more highly approve of members of Congress. Figure 6.1 provides evidence that they do not.

Clearing up this matter is important because previous research is in a muddle here. Almost universally, the expectation has been that educa-

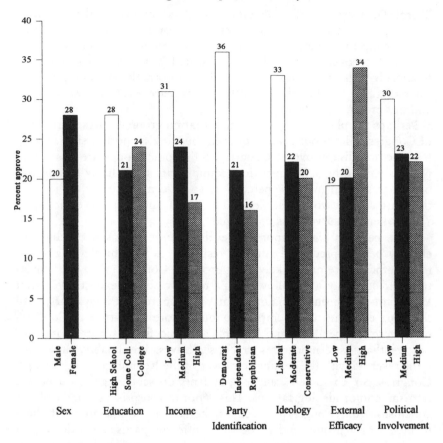

Figure 6.1. Approval of members of Congress

tion and support for Congress (or other legislative bodies, for that matter) would be positively related. For example, Patterson, Ripley, and
Quinlan speculate that educated citizens will be "more supportive of
institutions than the immiserated and unwashed" (1992: 319). Dennis
writes, "We would expect . . . that people high in education . . . would
be those most supportive of the existing set of political institutions"
(1973: 22). Patterson, Hedlund, and Boynton believe that legislative support will be "strongest among those high in levels of education" (1975:
56). Caldeira and Gibson see the education–institutional support
connection as so hackneyed that they refer to education as a control
variable (1992: 649). And Prothro and Grigg make like claims on the
basis of similar logic for the relationship between education and general
support for democratic principles (1960: 22).

Empirical findings, however, do not coincide at all with theoretical expectations. Among Ripley et al.'s sample of Ohio respondents, "variations in education levels do not appear to have an independent effect" (1992: 450). In fact, their coefficient is actually negative, though not significant. Summarizing results from a Harris poll, Davidson, Kovenock, and O'Leary note that "the better-educated Americans are among the most critical" (1968: 51). Then, turning to Gallup results, they are led to the same conclusion: "A larger proportion of the college educated were dissatisfied with congressional performance" (1968: 51). Dennis discovers a relationship between education and support, "with those *higher* in educational attainment being those *less* likely to be supportive of these institutions of government" (1973: 22). And Asher and Barr present NES data from the 1974 to 1992 period that demonstrate consistently that "more educated Americans were more likely to express disapproval of congressional performance than their less educated counterparts" (1993: 7).

The findings are hardly compatible with expectations and thus are worthy of attention. One possibility is that partisanship is contaminating the relationship between support for Congress and education and involvement. Maybe the reason educated and active citizens are less supportive of Congress is that Republicans tend both to have higher education levels and to be more involved in politics than Democrats (see, for example, Verba & Nie, 1972). Partisanship, then, may lie behind these puzzling findings. To see if this speculation has any merit, we broke down support for Congress by party affiliation and education, and then by party affiliation and involvement. The results are presented in Figure 6.2.

Controlling for party does not cause the puzzling negative relationships between education and congressional approval, and between political involvement and congressional approval, to disappear completely, but it does demonstrate where the negative relationships are concentrated. Among Democrats, it turns out, an approximation of the widely expected but elusive positive relationship materializes. Democrats with college degrees are more supportive of the Democratically dominated Congress than Democrats with less education. And Democrats who are highly involved in politics are about as supportive of Congress as those who are least involved (there is an odd curvilinearity to each of these patterns that we do not pretend to be able to explain).

But when the analysis is limited to just Independents or Republicans, those with more education and those more politically involved are actually less approving of the Democratically dominated Congress than their less educated or less involved cohorts. Part of the reason for these stubborn and possibly surprising relationships is that educated and in-

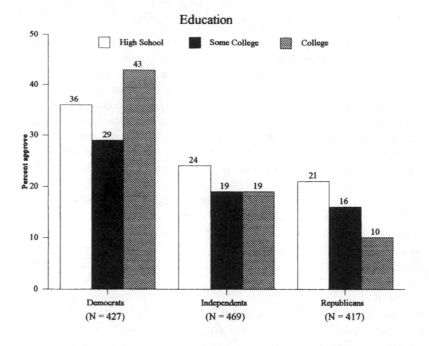

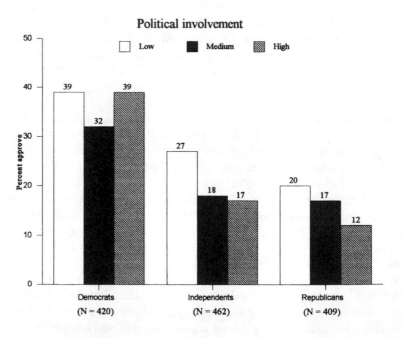

Figure 6.2. Party effects on approval with education and political involvement

volved Republicans and Independents were actually more likely to know that the Democrats were the majority party in Congress, and this knowledge made them more disapproving of Congress than their less educated fellow Independents and Republicans.[1] More generally, we believe, along with Davidson, Kovenock, and O'Leary (1968: 50–52), that educated people are more demanding and critical, and that they are more aware of missteps by members of Congress. Still, partisanship clearly plays an important mediating role in the relationship between support for Congress and education and involvement.

MULTIVARIATE ANALYSIS

We could go on forever, controlling for third and fourth variables, but the urge to do so is indicative of the need to present a full multivariate model. Such a model would allow us to investigate the influence of each independent variable while all the others are held constant, and would provide several other helpful diagnostics regarding the nature of these relationships and our overall ability to predict variations in approval of Congress.

General model

We begin, in simplest fashion, by entering the seven explanatory variables listed in Table 6.1 in a regression analysis with approval of members of Congress as the dependent variable. Unlike the bivariate correlations, we are now specifying a causal direction and are in a position to evaluate the effects of each independent variable while controlling for the others in the equation.

Conventional wisdom, though not our bivariate results, would lead us to expect that political involvement, income, efficacy, and education would all be positively related to approval of the members of Congress; that ideology and party identification would be negatively related since Republicans and conservatives, other things being equal, are likely to be less approving of the (pre-1995) Democratically dominated Congress;

---

1 Republicans are more likely to know which party controls the House (80 percent to 62 percent for both Democrats and Independents). Within partisan groupings, education has similar effects on knowledge of the majority party. Actually, Republicans increase the least with education, largely because they start from such a high level. Seventy-four percent of Republicans in the least educated category know the majority party, compared to 92 percent of the most educated Republicans, an eighteen-point difference. For Democrats, 80 percent of the most educated know the majority party whereas only 59 percent in the least educated category are aware of the proper answer. This is a twenty-one-point gap, and the gap for Independents is slightly larger (82 to 57 percent).

Table 6.2. *Approval of members of Congress: general model*

Variables	b	se	t
Sex	-.03	.01	-2.5*
Education	-.01	.02	-0.4
Income	-.10	.02	-4.0**
Party identification	-.12	.02	-6.2**
Ideology	-.03	.02	-1.8
External efficacy	.13	.02	8.7**
Political involvement	-.05	.02	-2.1*

$F_{(7,1092)} = 25.2$ Adj. $R^2 = .13$

Note: * $p < .05$; ** $p < .01$

and that women, perhaps, would be less approving of Congress because it is dominated by men, particularly prior to the 1992 election and subsequent to the Anita Hill–Clarence Thomas hearings.

The multivariate results in Table 6.2 allow us to confirm that conventional wisdom is inaccurate. While Republicans and conservatives are indeed less approving of Congress, and while efficacious individuals are indeed more approving, all the other conventional expectations are wrong. Gender, income, education, and political involvement are each negatively and (save for education) significantly related to approval of the members of Congress. This means that once we have controlled for the effects of efficacy, ideology, and party identification, the individual most likely to approve of the members of Congress has a low income, is female, is not politically involved, and possibly has little education.

These findings are quite surprising. With ideology and partisanship controlled, high-income males, having benefited from the political system, should be stronger supporters of that system and its component parts, including Congress. Educated and involved citizens should be more appreciative of the difficulties of governing. Since none of this is the case, an important message is conveyed. Dissatisfaction with Congress is not the province of inactive, uneducated, low-income malcontents. If anything, dissatisfaction is concentrated among groups of people who are involved with and who have benefited from the system.

We are again led to caution against the belief that increasing people's education about, and involvement in, the political system will improve perceptions of Congress. Our results provide another reason for worrying about the health of Congress. As Davidson, Kovenock, and O'Leary point out, "The manner in which the educated sector of the public views Congress is especially significant since these citizens tend to be the most active and most informed participants in political life" (1968: 51). What does it say about Congress when those who know it best and are the most involved with it are the least approving of it?

To us it says that, in this case at least, familiarity breeds contempt. People with more information about, and involvement in, the political system are more likely to know about the missteps of members of Congress, to expect more out of them, and to be disappointed with their performance. As a result, rather than being Congress's salvation, a more educated and involved population would do nothing to improve the public's opinion of it and may very well harm it.[2]

Adding the process variables

While the general model incorporates a fairly standard battery of variables, it ignores perceptions of government processes; these processes, we have argued, are at the center of public approval and disapproval of Congress. To test this contention, we created three variables. The first we call "democratic procedures"; it consists of respondents' perceptions of the importance of debate and compromise. Given the amount of debate and compromise in Congress, those people who do not value debate and compromise should be less approving of Congress.

The second variable measures attitudes toward professionalization of politics, and consists of respondents' sentiments toward the number of staffers in Congress, the degree of power concentration there, Congress's efficiency, and the degree to which members are perceived to concentrate on their world in Washington. If part of Congress's problem lies in some people disliking professionalization, then such people should be less approving of Congress, other things being equal.

Finally, we constructed a variable we call representation, consisting of

2 Some readers may be troubled by the fact that the dependent variable in Tables 6.2, 6.3, and 6.4 has only four possible values (strongly approve, approve, disapprove, and strongly disapprove). Using ordinary-least-squares estimation procedures in this situation is better than using it with a dichotomous dependent variable, but is still questionable. As a result, we repeated the analyses with a continuous dependent variable calculated by adding together each respondent's rating on the feeling thermometer with the equally weighted response to the approval question. The resultant variable ranges from 0 to 100 and is therefore perfectly appropriate for OLS. The results utilizing this modified dependent variable are very similar to those reported in our tables. Explanatory power is improved slightly, but the direction, relative size, and significance levels of the individual coefficients vary hardly at all from those we report in the tables.

Table 6.3. *Approval of members of Congress:
general model with process variables*

Variables	b	se	t
Sex	-.01	.01	-1.2
Education	.00	.02	0.1
Income	-.08	.02	-3.4**
Party identification	-.09	.02	-4.5**
Ideology	-.04	.02	-1.9
External efficacy	.05	.02	3.0**
Political involvement	-.00	.02	-0.0
Democratic procedures	-.01	.02	-0.5
Professionalization	.32	.05	7.0**
Representation	.27	.04	6.5**

$F_{(10,940)} = 34.9$ Adj. $R^2 = .26$

Note: $*p < .05; **p < .01$.

respondents' perceptions of the degree to which Congress is too heavily influenced by interest groups, fails to represent diverse groups, and has become detached from ordinary people. If some people believe decisions in Congress are reached in a procedurally unjust fashion, with certain groups being permitted a disproportionate share of influence, then those people should be less approving, ceterus paribus.

We added these three procedural variables to our general model. The results are presented in Table 6.3. The inclusion of these three variables has a notable influence on the explanatory power of the equation. Whereas the general model accounted for only 13 percent of the variance in approval of the members of Congress, the general model plus three procedural variables accounts for 26 percent of the variance. And of course this "increment to R^2" test underestimates the importance of procedure since it attributes any variance procedure shares with variables in the general model to those general variables.

What is more, two of the three procedural variables are in the expected direction, are highly significant, and are substantively important. Over and above the standard array of variables, perceptions of professionalization and of representational fairness make a big difference in predicting whether or not someone is going to approve of the members of Congress. The more that people dislike staffers and specialization, and the more that they believe Congress is not doing a good job representing all interests fairly, the more they disapprove of the members of Congress, even controlling for all the variables in the general model.

The one disappointment is the democratic-procedures variable. It is not statistically significant and, in fact, has the unexpected sign. Although we may be wrong about aversion to debate and compromise being part of the reason that the public dislikes members of Congress, there may be an alternative explanation. The questions available to us to measure support for such democratic procedures as debate and compromise are quite deficient. Asking people if they think debate and compromise should be an important part of what Congress is about does not address our belief that the public often reacts adversely to debate and compromise. Some respondents may say that debate and compromise are an important part of what Congress does, but these same respondents may not see members of Congress involved in these activities. Rather than seeing debate and compromise, respondents may see bickering and selling out. So even though Table 6.3 is unable to provide support for our view, we continue to believe many people are put off by debate and compromise *as they are practiced*, and that those who are most put off are the most likely to be dissatisfied with Congress.

But our results do buttress the view that perceptions of professionalization and procedural inequities contribute greatly to disapproval of Congress. In this sense, people are not happy with modern democratic procedures that tend to rely on professionalized politicians and professionalized institutions, and they are not happy with professional representation of societal interests that is often seen as representation only of special interests. On these last points the evidence is clear.

Approval of own member

One brief, final addition to the general model is in order. It is now commonplace to note the gulf between people's evaluations of Congress (what we now know to be the equivalent of evaluations of the members of Congress) and people's evaluations of their own member (see Fenno, 1975; Parker & Davidson, 1979). The public is truly fond of its own representative but quite unhappy with the collection of members. As noted in Chapter 3, about two-thirds of the respondents approved of their own member, whereas less than one-fourth approved of the congressional membership. These figures are consistent with those reported in earlier research.

Richard Born (1990) has made the useful point that just because levels of approval are quite different we should not conclude that support for our member and support for "Congress" are unrelated. The evidence he

Table 6.4. *Approval of members of Congress:*
general model with process variables and approval of own member

Variables	b	se	t
Sex	-.02	.01	-1.4
Education	.00	.02	0.1
Income	-.09	.03	-3.5**
Party identification	-.08	.02	-4.3**
Ideology	-.04	.02	-1.9
External efficacy	.05	.02	3.0**
Political involvement	.01	.02	0.3
Democratic procedures	-.03	.02	-1.2
Professionalization	.28	.05	5.9**
Representation	.23	.04	5.3**
Approve own member	.21	.03	7.5**

$F_{(11,833)} = 36.7$ Adj. $R^2 = .32$

Note: $* p < .05; ** p < .01$.

presents is consistent with the belief that there is some relationship between the two. We are in a position to determine whether or not evaluations of one's own representative can improve evaluations of Congress more generally. We do so by adding approval of member to the equation presented in Table 6.3. If Born is correct there should be a positive relationship between own-member evaluation and general evaluation.[3]

Table 6.4 does indeed provide support for the belief that evaluations of Congress are influenced by evaluations of one's own member of Congress. The coefficient for approval of one's member is positive, significant, and increases the explanatory power of the equation considerably (to .32, which is quite high for survey research). In fact, the regression coefficients suggest that evaluations of one's own member along with the two process variables described in the previous section are the most potent independent variables of the eleven now included in the equation.[4]

---

3 Of course, Born tends to think of the relationship as running the other way, with members' evaluations being influenced by general evaluations of Congress.
4 When a measure of the perceived distance in ideological policy space between the respondent and Congress is included in the model, it is in the expected direction

Who approves of Congress?

EXPLAINING APPROVAL OF CONGRESS
THE INSTITUTION

Support for the institution of Congress is not at all the same thing as support for the members of Congress. The correlation between approval of the institution and approval of the membership is .16, which means that, in the minds of the public, though they both have to do with Congress, these are two quite different referents. Thus, it would be a mistake to assume that the pattern of relationships described for evaluations of the institution of Congress will be anything like what we have for evaluations of the members of Congress.

In fact, Table 6.5 indicates just what a mistake it would be. Though the independent variables in this table are the same as those in Table 6.4, the dependent variable is now approval of the institution of Congress, and the relationships undergo a marked transformation. Women are more supportive than men of the members of Congress, but they are neither more nor less supportive of the institution. Approval of one's own member improves evaluations of the institution, though barely. Attitudes toward professionalization are positively related to evaluations of the institution, as they were to evaluations of the membership, but the other two process variables do not achieve statistical significance. Efficacy is one of the few variables behaving similarly for both referents, being strongly and positively related to evaluations of both the members and the institution.

The real changes come with regard to party identification and ideology on the one hand, and education and political involvement on the other. Party identification and ideology make a substantial difference in explaining variations in approval of the membership, but they are insignificantly related to evaluations of the institution. On the basis of our results, we can conclude that being Republican or conservative (in 1992) did not substantially decrease approval of Congress as an institution, even when Congress had been dominated primarily by Democrats for forty years.

But with regard to education and political involvement, the situation is in some respects the opposite. Whereas they were insignificantly and perhaps even negatively related to evaluations of the congressional membership, when it comes to evaluations of the institution of Congress, education and political involvement are strongly and positively related. In fact, along with feelings of efficacy, education and political involvement are the strongest predictors of approval of the institution.

(greater distance lowers approval) but is not significant at the traditional .05 level, although it would be significant at the more permissive .10 level.

Table 6.5. *Approval of the institution of Congress:*
general model with process variables and approval of own member

Variables	b	se	t
Sex	.01	.01	0.4
Education	.08	.03	3.1**
Income	.01	.03	0.3
Party identification	-.01	.02	-0.6
Ideology	-.02	.02	-0.9
External efficacy	.06	.02	3.3**
Political involvement	.12	.02	4.7**
Democratic procedures	-.01	.03	-0.2
Professionalization	.09	.05	1.8
Representation	-.01	.05	-0.1
Approve own member	.06	.03	1.8

$F_{(11,852)} = 7.7$ Adj. $R^2 = .08$

Note: $* p < .05; ** p < .01$.

Clearly, it is approval of the institution that behaves in the manner scholars originally expected, with more informed, involved, and efficacious citizens being more likely to approve of Congress as an institution. Evaluations of the membership, however, are quite a different story. Thus, the widespread expectation that support for Congress would be enhanced by greater education and political involvement is correct if we really mean support for the institution and not its membership. Our utilization of two distinct referents has made it possible to solve this long-standing split between conventional expectations and empirical findings.

We must continue to emphasize that the evaluations of the membership form the core of the public's evaluations of Congress. Determining the correlates of support for Congress as an institution is an interesting and useful endeavor, but should not blind us to the fact that in day-to-day terms, evaluations of the purely institutional component of Congress have little practical consequence. On the other hand, evaluations of the membership, particularly negative evaluations, have more concrete consequences, not the least of which is that they could lead to support for various proposals to reform Congress. We conclude this chapter by an-

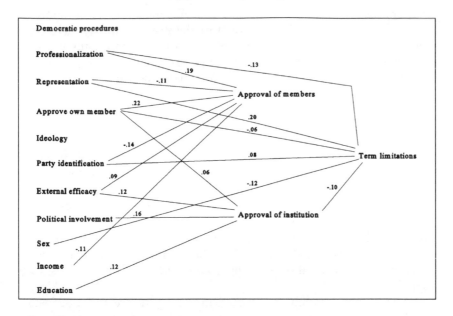

Figure 6.3. Support for term limits

alyzing the correlates of support for one of the more popular reforms of the early 1990s, the movement to limit the number of terms members of Congress are eligible to serve. Even if the ability of states to impose term limits on members of Congress is deemed unconstitutional, popular support for the concept continues as an intriguing topic of analysis.

TERM LIMITS

In Chapter 4 we analyzed in some detail the stability of support for term limits, but we made no effort to explain variations in support. We now turn to this latter task. Accounting for variations in our four-point scale for term limits, however, requires a slightly more involved model. This model is presented in Figure 6.3.

This figure reports the results of a path analysis, a technique made necessary since we know that our eleven independent variables affect approval of members and of the institution, since these two types of approval likely affect support for term limits (inversely), and since the independent variables may also have a direct effect on support for term limits. The model becomes even more complicated when it is recognized that approval of members has some (but not much) effect on approval of the institution, and that approval of the institution may have some (but not much) effect on approval of members (remember the bivariate correlation between approval for these two referents was only .16). This situation introduces a nonreciprocal feature to the equation and makes estimation somewhat more difficult.

As a result, we relied on a two-stage least-squares (2-SLS) estimation procedure in which the independent variables are used to predict approval of the members. Then this predicted variable (rather than the actual approval of members) becomes an independent variable when we attempt to account for variations in approval of the institution. The reverse procedure is utilized in explaining variations in approval of the members (for a fuller discussion of 2-SLS, see Asher, 1976: 59–61). As it turns out, the need for recognizing nonreciprocality is not great, since in the resultant fuller specification neither the relationship between approval of members and approval of the institution, nor that between approval of the institution and approval of the members, is statistically significant.

Regardless, the numbers reported in the figure are the 2-SLS standardized regression coefficients for each relationship that achieves traditional levels of statistical significance. Insignificant coefficients are repressed to avoid overloading the figure with lines and numbers. In this discussion, we focus primarily on the predictors of support for term limits since we have previously addressed the predictors of approval of members and the institution. The left side of the figure primarily reproduces the relationships discussed in previous sections of this chapter.

But the right-hand side provides some fresh insight into the variables that are related to support for term limits. Previous studies have attempted to identify groups most supportive of term limits to get a feel for the source of the reform pressure, but have not met with a great deal of success. John H. Fund reports a CBS/*New York Times* survey and quotes the political director of CBS News as saying that he had "never seen an issue on which there was so little demographic variation" (1992: 225). Rick Farmer notes conflicting findings in surveys on even so elementary a matter as whether partisanship is related to support for term limits (1993: 9). But he goes on to report results from a survey of Oklahoma City residents indicating that party identification and levels of alienation were important factors in explaining support for term limits. Uncertainty concerning who supports term limits clearly exists and needs to be addressed.

Our national survey tends to agree with Farmer's Oklahoma City sample but allows for a more complete discussion. Party identification is directly related to support for term limits, so even in this fairly elaborate model, with controls for most relevant concepts, Republicans are still more likely to support term limits. To some extent, limits were probably seen as a way to increase the number of Republicans in Congress prior to the 1994 change in partisan control, although Republicans may also have deeper philosophical reasons for supporting term limits. In this sense, it would be interesting to determine the extent to which Republican support for term limits was diminished by the elections of 1994. A similar though less expected finding has to do with gender. Women are significantly more likely than men to favor term limits even though they are no less likely to disapprove of either the general congressional membership or of Congress the institution. Our explanation is that many women see limits as a way to circumvent what appear to be barriers to the entry of women into Congress. Women's support for term limits is greater than would be expected in light of their attitudes toward members of Congress.

Respondents who are approving of their own individual representative, other things being equal, are less likely to support term limits, so again we see that a high approval rating for one's particular representative can be beneficial to Congress as it is currently structured.

Approval of the institution of Congress does affect support for term limits (negatively, as expected) but approval of the general membership, somewhat surprisingly, is not significantly related to support for term limits with other factors controlled. Finally, two of our three process variables have independent and direct effects on support for term limits. To the greater degree that respondents are bothered by the professionalization and perceived lack of just representation in Congress, the more likely they are to support term limits, even after other variables in the equation are controlled.

All told, support for term limits appears to be heaviest among female Republicans who are displeased with their own member, with Congress as an institution, and with the degree of professionalization and representational inequities they believe are present in Congress. Contrary to the conclusions of previous research, it is possible to specify the predictors of support for term limits. The proposed reform receives broad support, but this support is more heavily concentrated in certain portions of society. Part of the confusion in past research may stem from the fact that the motivations for supporting term limits are quite diverse, with one group viewing limits as a mechanism to reduce compositional inequities in Congress, another disliking professional politics of which extended terms is an integral part, and another perceiving a bias in the kind of representation provided by Congress.

CONCLUSION

Not only do people in general draw a distinction between Congress as an institution and its membership, but different variables help to explain support for each. Congress as an institution is most strongly supported by people who feel highly attached to, and part of, the political system; who are well educated; and who demonstrate interest and involvement in the system. On the other hand, the membership of Congress, at least when predominantly Democratic, is most strongly supported by the poor, by liberal Democrats, by the efficacious, and by people with less interest and involvement in politics. And it is the collective membership of Congress that people are reacting to when confronted with general questions about their feelings toward Congress. Just as baseball fans who have been involved with the game at some level may be the most demanding and critical observers of players, but also among the most loyal supporters of the game itself, political "fans" who are involved and knowledgeable may be demanding and critical of politicians even as they are supportive of political institutions.

We also discovered that approval of the institution and of the membership can be enhanced if respondents view their own representative favorably. Most important, we determined that perceptions of the manner in which Congress goes about its business, of its processes, are extremely influential in shaping attitudes toward Congress and its general membership. Even when other variables are controlled, perceptions that Congress is too professionalized and bureaucratized significantly harm evaluations of it. The same is true for perceptions that Congress is not procedurally just, that certain groups in society are treated better than others.

Process continues to matter when attention is turned to support for term limits – often seen as a reform championed by those who are disaffected with Congress. We find, as of the time of our survey, that it is not just Republicans who seek term limits, but also women of both parties, who are perhaps tired of the male hammerlock on congressional membership. In addition, regardless of party, people who believe Congress is too bureaucratic and professionalized, and who believe that it does not do a good job representing the interests of ordinary Americans, are more supportive of term limits. That public perceptions of process should continue to be so useful in explaining variations in support for Congress, as well as reforms designed to alter it, encourages us to address the nature and sources of these procedural concerns in more detail. This is the main task we pursue in Chapter 7.

7

Support for democratic processes

Democracy in the late twentieth century has such symbolic overtones and generates such strong positive emotions that it is easy to conclude that "Americans love democracy." Democracy is widely accepted as the best political system. To be called undemocratic is to be condemned. Indeed, "we live in a world that agrees on the importance and desirability of democracy" (Hanson, 1989: 68). Certainly, citizens of the United States are no different in this regard. But what is it that people love? What do people think is so desirable? We have argued thus far that Americans love democracy but hate democratic procedures.

Americans love the constitutional structure and the abstract principles underlying the political system in the United States. They strongly support the three national institutions and the constitutional structure itself. Other research also shows that Americans strongly value abstract democratic principles such as equality, liberty, and political involvement (Almond & Verba, 1963; McClosky & Zaller, 1984). So we can comfortably conclude that a vast majority of Americans love democracy.

But democracy does not begin and end with idealized structures and abstract principles. It also entails practices and processes that translate these structures and principles into real-world politics. Some of these processes must be present in all real-life democracies; others may be visible in only certain kinds of democracies or perhaps in an individual democracy at a particular time. For example, the democratic processes used in America today are not at all the same as those in place two hundred years ago. This point is vital because modern practices, though perhaps a necessary accommodation to the late twentieth century, are what people especially dislike. As we have seen, aversion to these processes contributes heavily to disapproval of Congress.

The analysis reported in the preceding chapter centered on the important overall effect of process evaluations on support for Congress. In this chapter, we recognize that process means more to some people than to others, just as policy or partisanship means more to some than to others. This recognition permits a more sophisticated model in which these varying orientations serve as conditioning variables in explaining the relationship between attitudes and institutional support. Similarly, we employ political expertise as a conditioning variable. Two people may have the same perceptions, but varying levels of political expertise could have a telling effect on how these perceptions are translated into support.

POLITICAL PROPENSITIES

We all know people who seem to see things from a clearly defined perspective. They interpret anything they hear or see in ways that reinforce their existing point of view. Their propensity to see the world in a certain way leads them consistently to make certain decisions and judgments. While some people seem extremely closed-minded, the fact is that everyone relies to some degree on existing attitudes to make decisions and judgments (Marcus et al., 1995). In fact, it is essential that we simplify the world around us in this way; otherwise we would be spending all our time trying to process – from scratch – every single bit of information. By relying on existing attitudes, we simplify our lives and have a better chance of making sense of what goes on around us.

Political scientists have long been interested in the implications of these belief systems for political judgments. Early research noted the role of ideology in the public's political evaluations (Campbell et al., 1960; Converse, 1964; Lane, 1962). People comfortable with ideological terms tend to think abstractly, to fit issues together in meaningful ways, and to hold stable positions on important issues of the day. However, this same research showed that few people are able to think ideologically, although Lane (1962) argued that people organize the political world in idiosyncratic ways and use their own singular belief systems to make sense of politics.

More recent research on belief systems is based on social cognitive psychology. Rather than focus on ideology, this stream of research examines the structure of attitudes and the way people process new information. Since politics is complex, people often simplify the political world around them by relying on certain biases, stereotypes, or frameworks to understand what is going on. These frameworks act to guide people toward certain types of information and away from other types, to emphasize certain concerns over others when making political judgments, and to interpret information in ways that support existing biases. By interpreting complex information in terms of an existing attitude structure, we limit the strain on our cognitive abilities and are better able to make sense of the world. Political scientists have most recently referred to these frameworks as attitudes structures, although they have also been called schemas, belief systems, and scripts.

When people obtain information about something – say, health care reform – they can interpret it in a variety of ways; that is, a number of belief systems may be relevant for interpreting this information. For example, if a person heard Hillary Rodham Clinton give a speech on health-care reform to a group of businesspeople, information could be interpreted in terms of the issue (health care), the deliverer (Hillary Rodham Clinton), the process of delivery (tone and characteristics of the speech), the political party of the deliverer (Democratic), Clinton's political role (head of the health-care task force), or the audience involved (businesspeople) (see Brody, 1986; Lau, 1986, 1989).

Research shows that, in interpreting the political world, people tend to rely heavily on just one dominant attitude structure, what we will call a propensity. When people hear something about politics, it is easiest to interpret the information by applying a frequently used framework. The reason for this, according to Erber and Lau (1990), is that these oft-utilized propensities are usually better organized, have stronger links to other attitudes, and are more easily accessible than other belief systems.[1]

What propensities are most relevant to a study of political attitudes? First, as we have argued throughout this book, people are attuned to *processes*, and perceptions of process color evaluations of Congress. Going one step further, it may be that certain people most often interpret the political world in terms of process; that is, certain people have a process propensity. When these people receive information about the government, they are likely to interpret the information in terms of processes, such as how the government functions, how decisions are made, how much power interest groups possess, how ordinary people fit in, how the electoral system functions, and so on.

Unfortunately, political scientists have largely ignored process considerations when studying public opinion. We think the reason for this oversight is the dominant place of vote choice in attitude research. Campbell et al. (1960) set the stage for future research by focusing on three variables relevant to vote choice: party, candidate image, and issues. This triumvirate has continued to dominate vote-choice research since that time.

The findings from the ensuing extensive research on the topic have been very useful, allowing us to learn a tremendous amount about how

1 Erber and Lau use the term "chronicity," which refers to the chronic use of a particular schema. We prefer "propensity" because it highlights the idea that people have a positive inclination to rely on a certain attitude structure rather than a recurring affliction.

people use partisanship, issues, and image to choose among candidates. When political psychologists turned to social cognition and information-processing theories, many continued to concentrate on party, issue, and image as the main pieces of information available to the electorate. For example, Erber and Lau (1990) focused on person and on policy propensities to get a better handle on political cynicism. They found that people with a strong person propensity became more cynical when dissatisfied with the incumbent president, whereas those with a strong policy propensity became more cynical when they felt alienated from the policy stands of the two major parties or candidates.

Scholars have also viewed party identification as an attitude structure. Since 1960, political scientists have considered party identification to be perhaps the most important perceptual screen Americans bring to politics. Identification with a particular political party, whether developed through childhood socialization (Campbell et al., 1960) or as the result of retrospective evaluations (Fiorina, 1981), is strongly related to vote choice and to other political attitudes. It seems likely that some people have a party propensity and, therefore, base their judgments on party identification. Party information is easily obtained, and identification with one party or the other often acts as a summary judgment of a wide range of issues and events, thereby simplifying the judgment process as a whole. When party labels or party cues are available, then, those with a party propensity can make quick and simple assessments.

We examine the propensities people display in their efforts to understand and to interpret politics, and argue that some people focus on those who inhabit certain political offices, some on political party affiliation, some on issues, and some on the processes of government. These propensities affect the kinds of information people react to and the evaluations they make. People weigh information differently and, therefore, may reach different judgments depending on whether they have a person, party, policy, or process propensity. The stronger a propensity, the more likely it is that any biases it promotes will be felt across a wide range of political judgments.

Measuring propensities

Researchers do not agree on how best to measure attitude structures, or propensities in particular, so they have relied on a variety of measurement methods, including experiments, intensive interviews, closed-ended questions on mass surveys, or open-ended responses on mass surveys. We have chosen to measure the four propensities by using open-ended questions from our national survey when possible and closed-ended questions when necessary.

We used open-ended questions to measure the person, policy, and process propensities. Early in the survey, respondents were asked the following questions: "Many people have been talking about the federal government lately. Please think about some good and bad points of the federal government. Is there anything you like about the federal government? Is there anything you dislike about the federal government?" Respondents were allowed to give up to three responses to each question, but we used only first responses to determine the person, policy, and process propensities.[2] First responses are the thoughts "at the top of people's heads" and, therefore, are more likely to reflect their propensity to think about politics in a certain way. People were then assigned to a propensity category only if they answered both the like and dislike questions using the same propensity.

Specifically, respondents were deemed to possess a person propensity if they answered both questions in terms of the members of the institutions, the job performance of people in government, specific public officials, or generalizations about politicians. Those assigned to the policy propensity answered both questions in terms of specific issues (domestic, foreign, economic, etc.). Respondents assigned to the process propensity were those answering in terms of the institutions of government, calls for the reform of certain processes, relations among the institutions, efficiency and organization, or specific processes such as those associated with elections or with the constitutional structure.

Party propensity was measured differently from the other three. The number of people who answered the open-ended questions in purely party terms was extremely small, in part, we assume, due to the nature of the question. Asking people what they like or dislike about the federal government does not readily call to mind, even for strong partisans, a direct reference to the political parties. Partisan responses are more likely to be embedded in other responses and therefore cannot be measured with the open-ended questions. Instead, we asked people to indicate their party identification in the survey, and further asked how strongly they identified with a party. We then assigned people to the party propensity if they indicated they were strong partisans and did not provide a person, policy, or process answer to both of the open-ended questions. The num-

2 Two political-science graduate students were provided with a list of codes and met with the authors to discuss in general terms the coding process. They then independently coded respondents' answers to these two questions. The intercoder reliability on these two questions was 93 percent. The coders then discussed the mismatches and agreed on the code to be assigned.

Table 7.1. *Characteristics of propensity groups*

		Propensities			
	Total	Person	Party	Policy	Process
N	1,433	143	66	359	195
Median Income	35–40,000	35–40,000	25–30,000	35–40,000	35–40,000
Mean Education	5.2	5.2	4.7	5.0	5.7
Mean Age	45	45	46	41	46
Sex:					
Female	54%	46%	67%	52%	53%
Male	46	55	33	48	47
Race:					
People of color	14	13	14	14	8
White	86	87	86	86	92
Efficacy:					
Low	36	50	30	39	33
Medium	36	33	31	37	35
High	28	17	39	24	32
Interest:					
Low	19	21	15	19	17
High	81	79	85	81	83
Party identification:					
Democrat	33	23	46	25	31
Independent	36	53	-	52	43
Republican	31	24	54	23	27
Ideology:					
Liberal	28	26		29	25
Moderate	28	33		29	36
Conservative	44	41		43	39
Political involvement:					
Low	30	30	28	34	26
Medium	37	38	34	42	39
High	33	32	38	24	35
Contact representative:					
No	46	45	57	53	37
Yes	54	55	43	47	63

Note: Education level: 1 = less than high school; 2 = some high school; 3 = high school graduate; 4 = some technical school; 5 = technical school graduate; 6 = some college; 7 = college graduate; 8 = postgraduate/professional degree.

ber of people in this category is small but presumably represents those who rely heavily on partisanship to make political judgments.

Characteristics of people in each propensity group

So who are the people who have a propensity to think about politics in party, policy, person, or process terms? A brief description may be helpful before proceeding to the heart of our analysis. Table 7.1 displays the characteristics of survey respondents within each of the four groups. It is clear, first of all, that the propensity groups are not made up of radically different types of people in terms of attitudes and demographics. People in the four groups share many characteristics, although some minor differences appear.

Respondents who think about politics in terms of the people in office tend to have less interest in politics and a low sense of external efficacy.

Half of the people in this group said they had a low sense of external efficacy, and only 15 percent called themselves highly efficacious. Respondents with a party propensity stand out more from the rest of the population. They tend to be poorer and less educated than the total sample, but they also tend to feel quite efficacious and interested in politics, to vote at a higher than average rate, and to consider themselves quite conservative (67 percent). Respondents with a policy propensity possess many of the same characteristics as those with a person propensity in terms of demographics, interest in politics, party identification, and ideology, although they are more efficacious and more likely to participate in politics.

Most notably, while not being totally unique, the process-propensity group stands out in several ways. These respondents are more highly educated than average and have high levels of efficacy, interest, and involvement in politics, matched only by those with a party propensity. People with a process propensity tend to be knowledgeable and involved in politics. They are more likely to discuss politics frequently and to contact their representative. They are engaged in the political system, both psychologically and behaviorally.

Some people relate to politics via policy, some via party, some via the people in government, and some via process. It is clear that these different propensities are not predetermined by demographic or attitudinal variables. At the same time, it is also clear that, particularly relative to those who see politics through policy or person lenses, those with a process propensity are more educated, efficacious, interested in, and involved in politics. As such, the process-propensity group is composed of citizens who are in a good position to make a difference (see Davidson, Kovenock, & O'Leary, 1968: 52). The connection of their perceptions with congressional support thus becomes a matter of more than passing importance.

Propensities and sensitivities

But this connection is not straightforward. It is not the case that a certain propensity automatically leads either to positive or negative evaluations of Congress. The percentage of respondents approving of Congress varies modestly across the four different propensities, with the person-propensity group the least approving (17 percent), the party-propensity group the most approving (36 percent), and both the process- and policy-propensity groups in the middle (25 percent for both). We had no strong theoretical reason to expect bigger variations across these groups.

We do, however, have a theoretical reason to expect that propensities act as weighting mechanisms. Two people may believe that Congress is significantly more liberal than they are in Left/Right policy space, but if one person has a policy propensity while the other does not, it is reasonable to expect that the policy-distance variable will be more telling for the person with the policy propensity. A parallel pattern could be expected for party, people, and process propensities. For example, if a person has a process propensity, then information about and perceptions of processes will be more important than the same information and perceptions would be for a person lacking a process propensity. The propensity indicates the kind of information that will be especially important to the individual making the judgment about Congress.

To demonstrate that this sensitizing notion is more than idle speculation, we use the process-propensity group to illustrate our point. If people hold a process propensity, their approval of Congress should be influenced more by process concerns than should that of those who hold either some other propensity or no propensity at all. Our empirical demonstration of this pattern employs the three components of modern procedures discussed elsewhere: democratic procedures (debate and compromise), professionalization, and representation. The results are presented in Figure 7.1.

If we are correct, we should see larger differences in approval of Congress among process-propensity respondents – depending upon their perceptions of the process – than among non–process-propensity respondents. In other words, the difference in approval ratings between process-propensity respondents who have a favorable assessment of process, and those with an unfavorable assessment of process, should be larger than the same difference among non–process-propensity respondents. We show these differences in Figure 7.1, where the matched columns for the process-propensity respondents should be more different from each other than the matched columns for the non–process-propensity respondents, thereby indicating a bigger "throw" for process variables if people have a process propensity.

This is precisely the pattern in evidence. Whether the respondents liked or disliked compromise and debate makes no difference in evaluations of Congress for those people lacking a process propensity. Twenty-five percent of those liking these democratic processes approve of Congress, as do 25 percent of those disliking these democratic processes. But for people with a process propensity, the story is slightly different. Twenty-three percent of those liking democratic procedures approve of Congress, but only 16 percent of those disliking democratic procedures do. This gap is not huge, but it is obviously greater than that exhibited by the non–process-propensity group. A process propensity does give additional weight to perceptions of compromise and debate.

Support for democratic processes

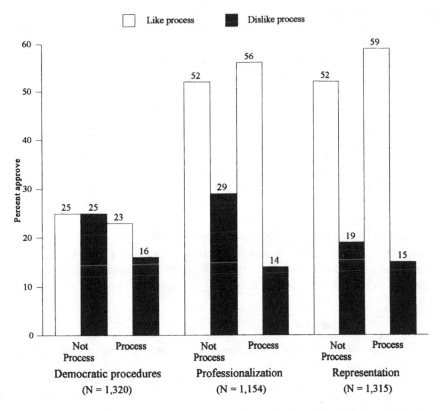

Figure 7.1. Process propensity and approval of members of Congress

The same pattern is evident with regard to attitudes toward political professionalization. Even if people do not have a process propensity, attitudes toward professionalization influence their approval of Congress. Fifty-two percent of those who favor professionalization are more approving of Congress, compared with only 19 percent of those who do not favor professionalization – a gap of 33 percentage points. This gap is even greater among respondents who give evidence of a process propensity: 56 percent to just 14 percent, a difference of 42 percentage points.

The story is similar for representation. Not surprisingly, people who perceive the members of Congress to be doing a better job of representing diverse interests are more approving of Congress, but the degree to which they are more approving depends upon their propensity. If they do not have a process propensity, the difference in approval rating is 52 percent to 19 percent (33 percentage points). If they *do* have a process propensity, the difference in approval is 59 percent to 15 percent (44 percentage points).

In each case, those with a process propensity weight process perceptions more heavily than those lacking one. We are pleased with this result because it indicates the important role propensities play in people's interpretation of political information. What is even more pleasing to us, however, is that process variables make a difference even for the majority of people who were not identified by our classification scheme as having a process propensity. Except for the (somewhat ill-suited) generic democratic-process questions, process perceptions matter for everyone. Those with a process propensity may be more sensitive to process perceptions, but this does not mean those lacking this propensity are oblivious to process. This finding confirms the results presented in the previous chapter concerning the importance of process perceptions in accounting for variations in people's approval of Congress. Even without a process propensity, process matters. With a process propensity, process matters even more.

Process propensities and congressional reform

Just as a process propensity heightens the ability of process perceptions to be translated into approval or disapproval of Congress, the propensity can also be expected to heighten the ability of process perceptions to be translated into support for or opposition to congressional reforms. To illustrate, we focus on two reforms about which we asked our national survey respondents, both of which involve what could generally be referred to as political professionalization or institutionalization.

Reducing both the salary of members of Congress and the length of time they can stay in office are wildly popular reforms and have been for quite some time. High salaries and lengthy careers in a body are integral parts of what we have been referring to as political professionalization, so it is only natural to presume that respondents who are more opposed to professionalization will be more supportive of reforms designed to reduce levels of it. Conversely, citizens who appreciate the need for professionalization could be expected to be less likely to support deprofessionalizing reforms such as term limits and salary reductions.

This much is obvious. However, we hypothesize that reform support of respondents who have been classified as possessing a process propensity will be more affected by these attitudes toward professionalization than will the reform support of those lacking a process propensity. We tested our hypothesis in a manner parallel to the procedures that yielded Figure 7.1, except that support for reform rather than approval of Con-

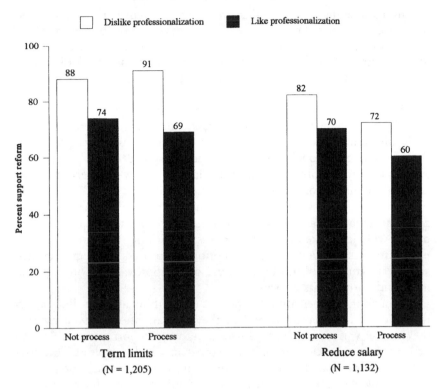

Figure 7.2. Process propensity and support for congressional reforms

gress now becomes the dependent variable. The results are displayed in Figure 7.2.

Just as people favorably disposed toward political professionalization are more approving of Congress, they also tend to be less willing to change the congressional status quo. In all four comparison pairs presented, the "dislike professionalization" group is always more eager to change Congress, whether by cutting salaries or by limiting terms statutorily. But we also find that, on the whole, people with a process propensity do not weight professionalization concerns quite as strongly in their reform support as we expected (although there are some differences).

The hypothesized ability of a process propensity to sensitize respondents to views of professionalization is less visible with regard to salary reductions for members of Congress than it is for term limits. For those lacking a process propensity, 82 percent of the group disliking professionalization favored a salary reduction, while 70 percent of those more willing to tolerate professionalization advocated cutting salaries, a difference of 12 percentage points. The process-propensity group was a little less supportive of cutting salaries and produced a similar gap across attitudes toward professionalization: 72 percent of antiprofessionalization respondents wanted a salary cut, while 60 percent of less antiprofessionalization respondents did.

When attention is turned to term limits, the expected pattern does materialize. For those without a process propensity, 88 percent of the antiprofessionalization group supported term limits, while 74 percent of the less antiprofessionalization group did, a spread of 14 points. The gap for the process-propensity group is larger. Ninety-one percent of the antiprofessionalization group wanted term limits, but "only" 69 percent of the less antiprofessionalization respondents advocated them, a gap of 22 percentage points. So a process propensity does not guarantee that people will either like or dislike process, but it does tend to encourage people to be sensitive to their perceptions of process. This greater sensitivity is manifested both in approval or disapproval of Congress and in attitudes toward its reform.

Although the propensities that people use to think about politics affect the kinds of information to which they pay attention as well as how they weight various kinds of information, other important variables can perform in similar capacities. The manner in which people think about politics is also related to the *amount* of information held, not just the type. People who know a great deal about politics may come to different judgments about democratic processes than people who know very little. We address the crucial role of political expertise in the next section.

POLITICAL EXPERTISE

People obviously differ in the amount of knowledge and interest they have in politics. Some people are highly knowledgeable about politics, knowing facts and having opinions on a wide variety of political issues, just as some people know everything about cars, cooking, backpacking, or baseball. Political experts often act as opinion leaders for those who are not terribly interested in politics. The differences between experts and those who know little about politics, called novices, are not always substantive. Experts are not necessarily more or less likely to be liberal or conservative, for example. Rather, experts and novices often simply think differently.

According to the literature, political experts differ from novices in several ways (see for example Schul & Burnstein, 1988; *Social Cognition*, 1990). First, experts have more complex attitude structures, which means they have more attitudes connected together in meaningful ways.

Support for democratic processes

Novices rely on one or two major organizing attitudes (say, party identification) that are often not connected to more minor attitudes. Experts
can rely on their major organizing attitudes or can branch off to smaller
but connected attitudes – say those concerning the relationship between
the president and Congress.

Second, experts have the ability to differentiate more finely within
categories because they are more likely to see distinctions between objects. For example, Born (1990) demonstrates that experts make separate
evaluations of Congress and their own member of Congress, whereas
novices evaluate the two as a unit. The political expert has a more complex cognitive structure concerning politics than does the novice and can
therefore pay attention to finer distinctions.

Finally, experts are highly involved in their cognitive processing; they
want to make "correct" evaluations. This means they are careful to focus
on highly relevant rather than superficial attributes and that they rely
more readily on past categorizations on which they know they can depend. Thus, experts and novices differ in how they make judgments and
think about politics.

While we are not in a position to provide empirical demonstrations
of all these anticipated consequences of political expertise, we can highlight a few of the ways expertise has important consequences for politics.
We will show that expertise encourages the adoption of certain propensities, that it influences people to be more or less favorable toward certain democratic processes, and that it sensitizes people to certain
perceptions. It appears that, in terms of overall evaluations of Congress,
expertise is a dual-edged sword: it increases the recognition of a need
for such legislative mainstays as debate and compromise but heightens
demands about the manner in which debate and compromise are conducted.

Theorizing about expertise and propensities

It is reasonable to expect that certain information levels will be associated with certain propensities. Of the four propensities discussed, thinking about politics in terms of party identification is probably the easiest.
Party labels are easily obtainable cues and can be used quickly to organize the political world. For example, a strong Democrat who sees the
Democratic party label attached to a candidate will react favorably even
if he or she has no other information. Thus, it is likely that novices will
be overrepresented among those with a party propensity.

Making judgments based on people in government is also easily accomplished. Research has shown that it is common for people to use
everyday information and information-processing techniques to make

political judgments (Popkin, 1991; Rahn et al., 1992); that is, we often think about politics in the same way we think about our everyday life, and this is especially true when we turn to thinking about people in government. We judge politicians using the same criteria by which we judge our neighbors or our friends. Again, this way of thinking about politics leads to quick, easy judgments and does not demand any special thinking about politics. We therefore expect novices to be more likely than experts to have a person propensity.

As far as issues are concerned, research has shown that sophisticated voters are more aware of and more likely than unsophisticated voters to base their votes on issues (Broh, 1973; Campbell et al., 1960; Smith, 1989). Gaining the necessary information to understand candidates' issue stands, for example, is difficult, and knowledge about pieces of legislation being discussed in Congress is equally – if not more – difficult to obtain. But Carmines and Stimson (1980) make an important distinction between easy and hard issues. Easy issues do not require much of an information base and are therefore easy for people to use. Hard issues require more complex information and are therefore more difficult to use. Since we did not make a distinction in our measurement of policy propensity between easy and hard issues, it may be that most people in the policy category think about politics in terms of easy issues ("I think we need to do something about crime" or "We really need to make the economy stronger"). Novices are likely to be overrepresented in the policy-propensity group when easy issues are involved, but experts are more likely to be overrepresented when hard issues weigh heavily in their thinking. Since few people rely on hard issues when making their judgments, we expect that the people in the policy-propensity category are relying more on easy issues and are less likely to be experts.

Finally, we come to the process propensity. We expect experts to be overrepresented in this category. While everyone is attuned to process to some extent, emphasizing process concerns to the point that they become a propensity demands that a person think about a variety of issues: how government works; the interrelationships among government institutions and among the people in them; the competing forces that influence government decision making; and the processes that best allow politicians to do their jobs. These concerns are not easy to think through and, thus, are likely to be the province of experts.

Various levels of expertise may also be related to the particular aspects of process that people think about and even favor, although such relationships are anything but simple. We would expect experts to be more understanding not only of the need for compromise and debate but also of the professionalization of the legislature and of efforts made to represent diverse interests, which frequently characterize modern democratic politics. But, on the other hand, experts are also likely to hold democracy to higher standards. Since experts themselves are relatively more aware of what goes on in politics, they may have loftier expectations and be more aware than novices of where members of Congress fall short of these expectations.

For example, experts may well recognize that Congress needs to become more professionalized to deal with modern problems, but they may also perceive Congress to be terribly inefficient and to use its resources unwisely. They may recognize that interest groups may theoretically need to play an important role in bringing interests before Congress but also believe that the current interest-group system does not fairly represent diverse societal interests. Thus, while experts may be more sensitive to the demands of modern democracy, they may see current democratic processes falling far short of their standards.

Determining the propensities of experts

To analyze the role of expertise we first needed to identify the experts and the novices among our respondents. In our survey, we asked respondents four general-knowledge questions, three of which were openended: "Can you recall who is head of the new Russian republic?"; "Do you happen to recall who is the secretary of state?"; and "Who is the secretary of defense?" The fourth question asked: "Is the current federal budget deficit larger or smaller than it was when Ronald Reagan first took office in 1981?" Correct answers were assigned a 1 and incorrect answers a 0.[3] We then created three categories: novices, who got no more than one answer correct (32 percent); a middle category of people who gave the correct answer to two or three questions (49 percent); and experts, who got all four questions correct (20 percent).

Table 7.2 shows that expertise is related to propensities. Similar percentages of novices and experts have a person propensity, but the other propensities show clear differences. More than twice as many novices than experts have a party propensity (14 percent of novices and 6 percent of experts). Novices are also much more likely to have a policy propensity (53 percent of novices and 36 percent of experts), apparently confirming our speculation about reliance on "easy" issues.

Most important, expertise is strongly related to having a process propensity. Experts are more than twice as likely as novices to rely on a

3 At the time of the survey, Boris Yeltsin was head of the Russian Republic, James Baker or Lawrence Eagleburger was secretary of state (President Bush reshuffled his cabinet during the time our survey was being administered), Richard Cheney was secretary of defense, and the budget deficit was larger than when President Reagan took office.

Table 7.2. *Expertise and propensities*

Propensities	Expertise		
	Novice	Middle	Expert
Person	18%	19%	20%
Party	14	6	6
Policy	53	48	36
Process	15	27	38
N	231	396	136
Process Subgroups			
Democratic Procedures	26	33	50
Professionalization	26	18	8
Representation	47	49	42
N	19	55	24

process propensity (38 percent of experts and 15 percent of novices). In fact, experts are more likely to hold a process propensity than any of the other propensities. Adopting a process propensity when thinking about politics demands greater cognitive reasoning and is therefore more likely to be adopted by political experts.

We also, however, can make a distinction within the process category among subgroups.[4] Some people in the process-propensity group focused on democratic procedures, some on professionalization, and some on representation. Which of these process subgroups are experts most likely to turn to when thinking about the federal government? Table 7.2 again shows a striking difference among expertise groups. Both novices and those in the middle category heavily emphasize representation: the ability of interest groups to influence the federal government and the degree to which ordinary people are being represented. Fully half of the experts, however, emphasize democratic procedures when thinking about the federal government. Their answers concern the relationship between the

4 When analyzing specific subprocesses, respondents could qualify by only mentioning the subprocess concern in response to the dislike question because we needed to have a sufficient number of cases. For the larger group analysis, as described in the text, we were able to demand that respondents respond in terms of process to both the like and dislike queries.

Table 7.3. *Expertise and attitudes toward democratic processes*

Democratic Process Variables	Expertise		
	Novice	Middle	Expert
Democratic procedures			
Low	42%	43%	28%
High	58	57	72
N	441	679	281
Professionalization			
Low	82	86	89
High	18	14	11
N	368	579	258
Representation			
Low	77	86	88
High	23	15	12
N	429	684	281

president and Congress, the need to compromise on issues, and so on. Only 8 percent of experts emphasize professionalization.

Expertise and attitudes toward democratic processes

We can further understand the relationship between political expertise and process by looking at how favorably novices and experts, respectively, react to the three specific process variables discussed in the last chapter. Here the focus is not on the kinds of propensities adopted by experts but on whether they are favorably or unfavorably disposed toward particular processes. Table 7.3 provides evidence that experts are much more positive about democratic procedures than are novices. In fact, 72 percent of experts rate debate and compromise as a very important part of the job representatives do; only 58 percent of novices rate it that high.

But experts are also more critical of the professionalization of the legislature and of the representative function of legislators. Among experts, 89 percent are highly negative toward professionalization and 88 percent toward representation, compared to 82 percent and 77 percent, respectively, for novices. This finding is worthy of some emphasis. Political experts, as might be expected, are more likely to recognize the importance of debate and compromise to democratic government. But they are not more likely to be tolerant of political professionalization and modern styles of interest-group involvement. Experts are not opposed to all democratic processes; they tend to be upset with professionalized politicians and professionalized interest-group representation. It is a certain style of democratic processes rather than all democratic processes that seems to bother political experts. Novices, on the other hand, are less likely to condemn professionalization and representation, but are also less supportive of debate and compromise.

Expertise and sensitivity to perceptions

Just as we anticipated that propensities would sensitize people to relevant variables, we also expect that political expertise will lead relevant variables to have more consequence. We tested this expectation in a format similar to that evident in Figure 7.2, but this time we looked at whether expertise (not a particular propensity) leads to greater differentiation in support for reforms. More specifically, since term limits and salary reductions are both reforms that would diminish current levels of political professionalization in Congress, it is likely that those respondents most bothered by professionalization will be the most supportive of the reforms. But attitudes toward political professionalization should make more of a difference among experts, who are basing their views on more information, than among novices.

Figure 7.3 indicates that expertise has precisely the expected effect. Compared to novices, experts are much less supportive of lowering the congressional salary, but their views are also more contingent upon their beliefs about professionalized politics. Sixty-three percent of experts who dislike professionalization support salary reductions, compared to only 36 percent of experts who are less negative toward professionalization. The spread for political novices is only 91 percent to 83 percent.

A much less dramatic contrast is apparent for term limits. Attitudes toward professionalization alter support for term limits by 19 percentage points among political experts and by 16 percentage points among political novices. Support for term limits is strong, even among those who are not all that opposed to political professionalization. But the larger message is that political expertise does have the expected sensitizing effect in support for congressional reform and, we would anticipate, numerous other variables.

Support for democratic processes

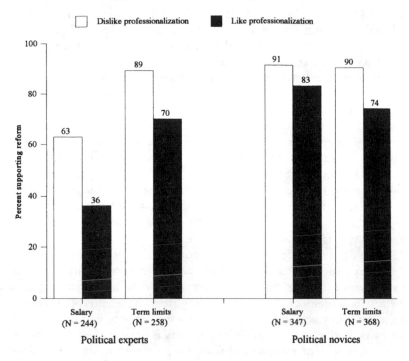

Figure 7.3. Expertise and support for congressional reforms

So, being an expert in politics does affect how one thinks about politics. First, experts can think about politics in a more complex way and are able to rely on process concerns to guide their political judgments. Novices, on the other hand, predominantly rely on issues – particularly easy issues – when thinking about politics. Second, experts are more favorably disposed to compromise and debate; this much is encouraging. But they are not predisposed to be supportive of political professionalization or the visibility of interest groups in modern American politics. Finally, political expertise sensitizes people to give more weight to relevant information when determining whether or not to be supportive of such things as political reform.

CONCLUSION

Political scientists have all but ignored the study of process in favor of focusing on candidate image, issues, and party. The reason for this focus is obvious: all three variables contribute to people's vote choice. By so heavily emphasizing vote choice in political-behavior research, political scientists have not addressed other important considerations in people's political judgments. We think it is time to redress this negligence.

We found in the last chapter that process concerns are strongly related to evaluations of members of Congress. In this chapter, we have tried to determine the kind of person most likely to think about politics in terms of processes. Not only do most people take into account process concerns in their evaluations, many actually think about politics predominantly in process terms. When confronted with political information, some people are most influenced by process considerations and use perceptions of process to make judgments about the political world. People with a process propensity tend to be sensitive to process variables when making political judgments (concerning such things as approval of Congress and support for specific congressional reform proposals). This statement is almost definitional in theory, but it is comforting to report that it is supported by our data.

Another potent difference among people is their level of expertise. Just as the way people think about politics varies with propensity, so too does it vary with expertise. Political experts tend to be more concerned than novices about democratic processes, they are more sensitive to certain variables, and they are both more and less supportive of certain democratic processes. Perhaps our most chilling finding is that 35 percent of political novices approve of members of Congress, 21 percent of those between novices and experts approve, and only 18 percent of political experts do. Increasing knowledge of politics seems to go along with decreasing support for members of Congress (though not when Congress is conceptualized in purely institutional terms – see Chapter 6).

While our subsequent probings do not transform these numbers into a cheery finding, they do allow us to explain why it exists. Experts are, in fact, more appreciative of the importance of debate and compromise (what we are calling democratic procedures) to a democracy. If this were the end of the story, experts would probably be more approving of Congress, but it is not. Experts are more likely than novices to be disturbed by the professionalized and representationally skewed procedures visible in Congress. Our explanation is that experts are more demanding and more aware of shortcomings. Experts are more likely to appreciate the need for possibly raucous debate and unsatisfying compromises in a democracy. They are not convinced, however, that the particular democratic processes currently on display in the American polity are working. Such an attitude among the very best-informed citizens is dripping with implications, and the existence of this attitude among this important group will play a central role in our efforts in the final chapter to synthesize our findings and suggest how public attitudes toward political bodies such as Congress could be improved.

8

Conclusion:
The people and their political system

We see a need for reorienting the way political observers consider and conceptualize public opinion and political institutions. Researchers have traditionally treated public opinion and governmental institutions as distinct entities. What little overlap they concede usually places institutions in a peripheral or marginalized category by focusing either on vote choice, which shapes the membership of the institutions, or on the congruence of views between constituents and governmental officials within a narrow policy area. Yet the relationship between citizens and their governmental institutions is much more than this scholarship allows. The relationship, properly conceived, includes how people feel about their institutions, what they like and dislike, proposed changes they support and oppose, and the way the institutions interact with people like them. The research reported in this book constitutes an attempt at analyzing this larger relationship between public opinion and governmental institutions. What have we found?

IT'S THE PROCESS, STUPID

Discussions of public opinion have usually pertained to voting behavior, and thus have detailed the public's evaluations of specific candidates in terms of policy concerns, partisanship, and perceptions of candidate image. When the dependent variable is evaluation of a branch of government rather than of an individual, however, another variable must be added to the mix. This variable is process, and it has been at the heart of our presentation. People's views of the political system and of particular bodies within that system are shaped not just by policy outcomes, by the image of certain individuals, or by partisan loyalties, but primarily by the processes employed in the system and in the institutions.

The intense reaction to the Clarence Thomas–Anita Hill episode was not driven by the final product, the confirmation of Judge Thomas, but was instead traceable to public perceptions of how the process unfolded, to the handling of Professor Hill's allegations, to the composition and comportment of the Senate Judiciary Committee, and to the questions they asked as well as how they asked them. Process, particularly the more visible aspects of it, is what most ordinary people care about. It is what they relate to. People often have understandable difficulties comprehending the substantive complexities of issues, but they can react to certain groups getting more influence than others, to undeserved privilege, to sloth, and to what they interpret to be self-interested motivations. These factors are salient to most ordinary people, the items with which they resonate.

Given the centrality of process, the key task is to determine the particular processes the public holds in favor and in disfavor. What do our results tell us about this crucial matter? To no one's surprise, Americans dislike the kind of democratic processes believed to be practiced in Washington these days. Such practices are inefficient, they think. Large staffs, mossback politicians, and oversized benefits packages seem to be of no assistance in the government's ability to deal with pressing national problems in an expeditious and straightforward manner. In the minds of the people, the professionalized political institutions of today are not contributing to efficient resolutions; perhaps modern accoutrements have even made the situation worse by conveying the sense of a ponderous, expensive, massive, and largely unresponsive system. The public sees dawdling where it wants to see action.

Such practices are also inequitable, people think. Certain interest groups are given more access than others. With access comes influence. As a result, governmental decisions are not rendered in a procedurally just fashion. The public's undifferentiated view of interest groups exacerbates the perception, setting up an "ordinary people versus special interest" contest. There are those groups with money who can hire lobbyists and can play the Washington game, and there are the rest of us. They have influence and we do not. As a result, ordinary people are being ignored. The process is not just.

In the case of both professionalization and representation, people clearly are upset. Inefficiencies that appear pointless are frustrating, especially when important problems are seemingly ignored. Inequities owing to wealth and access create disillusionment, especially when the common sense of ordinary people is perceived to be treated in a cavalier manner. Overprofessionalization and inequitable representation swirl together in the minds of the people, producing a vision typified by lobbyists and members of Congress traveling together to warm golf vacations or lavish ski retreats. The people are disgusted with this style of democratic procedure.

Conclusion

But our focus-group research shows, and the findings from our national survey support the idea, that people do not distinguish between essential modern democratic processes and perceived abuses of those processes. People often have a gut reaction to process concerns, lumping anything having to do with process into one large "bad" category, rather than making important distinctions. (This reaction to process contrasts with reactions to structure, to the Constitution, and to static institutions, which are quite favorable.) For example, we found that any mention of interest groups raises people's ire. They do not recognize that some interest groups might be good, that their own interests are represented by some interest groups, or that interest groups can play a useful role in the political system. To our respondents, interest groups are invariably evil, and Congress's members are evil for being in any way associated with them. People's responses to any mention of perquisites and professionalization are similarly visceral. People believe no job benefit is truly deserved these days. In essence, people's perceptions of professionalization and representation in a modern democracy are indiscriminately negative. Because the process occasionally misfires, many people seem to doubt completely the engine's viability, and at times unrealistically yearn for what they see as the idealized days of the horse and buggy.

So together, modern professionalized politicians and modern professionalized interest-group representation form a deadly mix in the public mind, contributing greatly to dissatisfaction with the political system. But we fear that the problem runs deeper than dissatisfaction with perquisites and special interests. A surprising number of people, it seems, dislike being exposed to processes endemic to democratic government. People profess a devotion to democracy in the abstract but have little or no appreciation for what a practicing democracy invariably brings with it. The focus-group evidence supporting this contention was overwhelming (although unfortunately our survey questions were not suitable for providing confirmation). People do not wish to see uncertainty, conflicting options, long debate, competing interests, confusion, bargaining, and compromised, imperfect solutions. They want government to do its job quietly and efficiently, sans conflict and sans fuss. In short, we submit, they often seek a patently unrealistic form of democracy.

Process is important to people, and people are less than realistic about the kind of process they can have while remaining within the strictures of modern democratic government. It may or may not be unrealistic to think this process can exclude governmental and interest-group professionalization, but it is definitely unrealistic to think it can exclude diversity, mess, compromise, and a measured pace. Like public opinion in so many other areas, the people want it both ways. Not only do they want lower taxes and more services, they also want democracy and no mess. This combination of beliefs frequently leads to disappointment. It is not the case, however, that this disappointment is spread evenly across all governmental institutions.

VARIATIONS ACROSS INSTITUTIONS

If we are correct that the public is particularly upset with professionalized government, with special-interest influence, and with torpid debate and unfulfilling compromises, it stands to reason that approval of institutions will covary with the extent to which institutions display these traits. The structure, orientation, norms, and visibility of the three institutions of the federal government differ tremendously, and these differences evoke fundamentally different reactions from citizens.

The Supreme Court has an enormous advantage over the other political institutions. Justices have low profiles in the minds of most Americans; moreover, they are seen in dignified settings, never arguing with each other or cavorting with lobbyists on Caribbean beaches. In late 1993, one associate justice of the Supreme Court caused a minor stir just by giving a speech to a group perceived to be ideological. This is a far cry from members of Congress, who interact daily with interests of an intensely ideological sort. As a result, most citizens do not distinguish between members of the Supreme Court and the Court itself. Moreover, the Court is associated with the constitutional system but is viewed as being above the Washington system; decisions seem firm and clear, with bickering and deal making sheltered from the public view, notwithstanding an occasional aberration or exposé.

While the presidency does not have the same advantages as the Supreme Court, it does have several. Not the least of these is that it is organized in a hierarchical fashion. Administrations occasionally break out into disagreeing factions with conflicting leaks, spins, and jabs, but these rarely register with citizens. The incidents are also softened by the sense many disputants have that when a decision has been made, the wagons should be circled and a reasonably unified front presented. Internal disputes are not routinely publicized in a forum likely to permeate the public consciousness. Ordinary people do not see members of the administration openly disagreeing, although the attentive public may be aware of such events. The "person at the top" structure gives a sense of order and perhaps even movement to the presidency.

Congress is the most disadvantaged institution since it lacks the secrecy of the Supreme Court and the hierarchical structure of the presidency. It is an open, collegial body with substantial power. Given the responses we obtained in our survey and our focus groups, this clearly is the perfect recipe for disrespect. The American public has little stomach for uncertainty and equivocation, for bargaining and politically expedient compromise, for extended talking and partisan bickering, and this is exactly what Congress is about. Members of Congress are not able to ban the public from most internal debates, as is the Supreme Court. They are not able to ask the press to leave once photo opportunities have been provided. Efforts at working out solutions to problems are public to a fault. Congress is an enemy of the public *because* it is public. As the most public institution, it acquires the inside track for being the least liked institution.

Seen in this light, some might wonder why Congress was ever liked. But the evidence that Congress was once liked is weak. As noted in Chapter 2, approval of Congress has never been consistently high, occasionally blipping up but never remaining there for anything approaching a sustained period. The slight downward trend prior to 1995 is easily incorporated by our explanation. Congress has become even more open and exposed in recent decades. The press has been more probing, investigative journalism is more prevalent, sessions are now televised, and media gatekeepers consider few events to be out of bounds. The clubbish, quiet, insider-dominated institution has been replaced by a decentralized, media-oriented one (Polsby, 1975). Whereas decisions used to be made over bourbon and branch water in Sam Rayburn's office, and media hounds were viewed with suspicion, decisions now seem to be made under klieg lights or on radio talk shows, and the quiet members are left behind. Congress has changed. Whether for better or for worse is not the issue right now. What is clear is that these changes have fanned the flames of public dissatisfaction.

A similar trend is evident for other legislatures in the United States. Alan Ehrenhalt offers a wonderful account of what has happened in many state legislatures.

The legislatures of a generation ago . . . were, to put it bluntly, racist, sexist, secretive, boss-ruled, malapportioned and uninformed. But there was no great public outcry against any of those conditions. The Alabama legislature, ranked in a Ford Foundation study in 1971 as 50th out of 50 in independence, 50th in accountability and 48th in overall performance, had been judged favorably just three years earlier by 65 percent of the respondents to a statewide poll. In 1990, freed of its racism, secrecy and malapportionment, fully equipped to gather information and operating in a new, state-of-the-art legislative facility, it got an approval rating of 24 percent. (1992: 30)

At first blush, the combination of improving legislatures and declining public approval of those legislatures is difficult to understand. But in light of our account of what the public likes and dislikes, this combination is exactly what should be expected. The public, regardless of its protestations, does not like visible, professionalized legislatures, so when legislatures come out of their shells and become more professionalized and visible, public approval can be expected to diminish (see also, Jewell, 1982: 179–181; Squire, 1993). It does.

And residents of the United States are not distinct in their contempt for modern legislative bodies; the attitude is global. It is particularly instructive to see dissatisfaction with national legislatures so prevalent in the new democracies of Central Europe (see, for example, Hibbing & Patterson, 1994). Public-opinion polls in the new democracies show that it is common for people being exposed at close range to democratic procedures for the first time to recoil instinctively, and for them to recoil most from legislatures, since that is where these procedures are most evident. These new legislatures have been referred to as nothing but "rowdy debating societies" (Perry, 1990: 4). The needed next step is to recognize that rowdy debating societies are precisely what legislatures are supposed to be. They are supposed to debate, and it is not unusual for debate to become animated as the members try their best to reflect the intense feelings present in society on certain issues.

But Congress wields more power within the U.S. government than nearly any other national legislature wields within its system. The American people, certainly, believe that Congress is far more potent than the presidency and the Supreme Court (see Chapters 3 and 5). As a result, whenever people are dissatisfied with a governmental policy or even a societal condition that may or may not be tied to governmental action, they tend to blame Congress. In addition, the clout of Congress increases pressure on it to professionalize so it can address the problems it confronts, but this clout also makes Congress an unusually attractive target for special-interest petitions. Congress has the typical burdens associated with open, collegial institutions, and it has the extra burdens associated with a body believed to be able to make a difference on its own. Congress, like other legislative bodies, is vulnerable; more than other legislative bodies, it is culpable.

The perceived power of Congress also means that evaluations of it will be particularly influential in shaping citizen evaluations of the overall political system. People may be reasonably positive toward the president or the Supreme Court, but if these institutions are perceived to be much less central than Congress, and if Congress is viewed negatively, attitudes toward the overall governmental system may very well be negative. In essence, the perceived influence of Congress causes the consequences of attitudes toward it to be magnified.

Conclusion

VARIATIONS ACROSS PEOPLE

But not all people possess the attitudes we have described. Not all people dislike Congress. Not all people dislike professionalization, think special interests are inherently evil, and are disturbed by the specter of democratic procedures. These attitudes are typical, but substantial individual variation occurs around them. By accounting for these variations we are able to acquire information on the source of public attitudes toward political institutions and the political system more generally. This was our main goal in Chapters 6 and 7.

The people who support Congress the institution are not the same as those who support Congress the collective membership. Before we directly address these differences, it is important to keep in mind that when people are asked about the generic "Congress," they actually respond in terms of the membership of Congress, not the institution. An obvious implication of this finding is that if we want to determine people's attitudes toward *Congress*, focusing on support for the *institution* is less important than focusing on support for the *membership*.

Nonetheless, public attitudes toward Congress as an institution offer an instructive contrast to evaluations of Congress as a collection of members. Much research has posited that more-educated people should be more supportive of Congress, but empirical results have not confirmed this contention. In our research, education is significantly related to support for the institution of Congress, as are political involvement and efficacy. Thus, the most favorable attitudes toward the institution emanate from educated, involved, and efficacious individuals. Party and ideology, on the other hand, are not related to purely institutional evaluations.

In many respects, this pattern of results is the opposite of what we observed for the congressional membership. The membership of Congress is most likely to be viewed unfavorably by Republicans, as could be expected given the dominance of Democrats in Congress at the time of the survey. But even with partisanship controlled, income, political involvement, and educational attainment are still either negatively related or not related at all to approval of the membership.

The inability of education and political involvement to encourage support for the membership is striking. The results persist under a variety of specifications, and are consistent with a good deal of the previous empirical research on support for Congress (see Asher & Barr, 1993). So we believe the results are real and need to be explained, especially in light of our finding that education and involvement are positively related to support for the institution. Our explanation is that people who are more knowledgeable and involved with politics are highly supportive of the standards established by the Constitution, but are more demanding of politicians and more aware of their shortcomings because their expectations are high.

If approval of the congressional membership is not enhanced by education or political involvement, what increases approval? Or perhaps we should more appropriately ask what feeds public disapproval. Consistent with the theme of this book, process variables are powerful. Those respondents most negative toward professionalized government are most negative toward the congressional membership. And those perceiving the representational process as being tilted toward special interests are also the most negative toward the congressional membership, even after controlling several other variables. Our more general democratic-procedures variable did not behave as predicted, but on the whole it is apparent that perceptions of democratic processes are important determinants of congressional-membership approval.

Because of the importance of process preferences and perceptions, we attempted in Chapter 7 to explore in more detail the nature of process-based attitudes. We found that not only do process variables affect people's evaluations of Congress, but that there is a fairly large subset of people who actually have a propensity to think about politics in process terms. Because of their emphasis on process concerns, these people give greater weight to process information when evaluating Congress or reform proposals. The extent to which they are favorable or unfavorable toward democratic procedures, professionalization, or representation has a larger impact on their approval of Congress and on support for reforms than is true for people who think about politics differently. Even so, those without a process propensity still take the process variables into account when evaluating Congress, just not to the same extent.

We also found that examining political expertise sheds significant light on our understanding of democratic processes. Experts are more likely than nonexperts to have a process propensity, presumably because they are better able to think through complex process concerns. Experts also tend to take more extreme stands on our three process variables: they are much more likely to favor debate and compromise, and much more likely to oppose professionalization and current forms of representation than novices. Finally, experts give greater weight to the process variables in their evaluations and preferred reforms of Congress than do novices.

The key point is that process concerns are varied, important, and often neglected by analysts. Process concerns play a highly significant role in people's evaluations of Congress, and also constitute the primary way some people think about politics. Experts, the most politically knowledgeable and active segment of society, are more likely to hold a process propensity than any of the other propensities we considered. Experts often act as opinion leaders, which significantly increases the importance of their emphasis on process.

INCREASING CONGRESSIONAL APPROVAL

Detailing reasons that some people are more negative toward Congress than others does nothing to obviate the fact that, in toto, popular sentiments toward Congress are *decidedly* negative. In light of our results, what, if anything, can be done to diminish this negativity?

Changing congressional procedures

If we are correct about process being at the core of public dissatisfaction, the simple answer to the preceding question would be, "Alter congressional procedures." Certainly, many of those dissatisfied with Congress have gravitated toward various reform proposals, particularly term limits; accordingly, we have addressed the nature and correlates of term limits in Chapters 4 and 6. But now is the time to reflect upon how reform is likely to alter support for Congress. We provide evidence that people are upset with both the professionalization of Congress and the influence of special interests there. In fact, we tied these attitudes together under the notion that people were unhappy with the Washington system.

This being said, perhaps the way to improve the public's image of Congress is to reduce professionalization and special-interest influence. The public is ecstatically supportive of reforms so directed: term limits, staff reductions, salary reductions, reduction of committee power, reduction of the power of parties and party leaders, campaign-finance reform (though not public financing), gift-giving restrictions on lobbyists, banning paid lobbyists, outside-earnings limits, eliminations of office perquisites, and so forth. Should the public be given what it wants?

To some extent. The powers that be should be more willing to consider the effects of reform on public opinion. An example of members of Congress taking public opinion into account occurred in the debate on banning lobbyist gift giving. According to Senator Carl Levin (D.-Mich.), "This will make a major contribution to increasing public trust in the institution" (quoted in Seelye, 1994: A9). Indeed, when enumerating the benefits of a proposed reform, that the people overwhelmingly desire the reform should not be ignored. After all, the people should have some say in the structure of the people's branch. It is wrong to dismiss out of hand popular reform proposals just because they may seem silly to institutional insiders. In a democracy, the people have a right to be silly.[1]

At the same time, popular views should not automatically be determinative. When enumerating the liabilities of a proposed reform, the consequences for the institution should not be ignored. By drafting the Constitution as they did, the founders indicated a greater concern with protecting against structural silliness than policy silliness. Most changes in process require supramajorities at multiple stages since they entail constitutional amendments. Policy changes can be much more easily put into effect, usually requiring only a simple majority. While we have argued that the public's reform agenda needs to be taken more seriously by those close to Congress, the obstacles in the way of a populist rush to deprofessionalize Congress into a pastoral, citizen legislature should not be removed.

Why not? For one thing, the public demonstrates little understanding of the difficulties facing government in the complex, modern world. There may be abuses of democratic processes, but people also prefer to ignore crucial facts such as (1) we ask government to do much these days, and a substantial governmental infrastructure is necessary to meet these demands; and (2) public opinion is divided on many issues, and interest groups attempt to represent these different views when dealing with governmental officials. The public's favorite reforms are based on the desires to turn the clock back on professionalization and to banish interest groups. But it is likely that these reforms would only improve the public's outlook on Congress in the short run. In the long run, it could be argued, these same reforms would render Congress less able to deal with increasingly difficult and divisive problems in the efficient manner desired. Public opinion should be part of the calculus, but so should the capacity of the institution to fulfill its constitutionally specified roles in a changed and changing world.

More telling, if we are correct about people's aversion to overt demonstrations of democratic processes, it is obvious that reforming the political system to give the people what they want structurally can be taken only so far, assuming we want to preserve these processes. But evidence

1 When the Joint Committee on the Organization of Congress held its hearing in early 1993, virtually no truly public input became part of the record. Of the 243 people who testified, 170 were members of Congress, 15 were congressional staffers, and 44 were "outside experts," usually political-science professors or individuals affiliated with think tanks (actually, less than 44 were "outside experts," since some testified more than once). H. Ross Perot claimed to speak for the people, though the views of an individual whose annual income is so many standard deviations above the mean probably should not be taken for those of the people. Perhaps this skewed distribution of witnesses is why the agenda of the Joint Committee was, by the standards of the public, tepid.

for this particular alleged aversion is open to challenge. The issue represents one of the very few instances in which our survey results were somewhat inconsistent with those of our focus groups. Whereas focus-group respondents went on at some length criticizing debate, compromise, and inefficient decision making, the survey results did not indicate that people more taken with the importance of debate and compromise were actually more approving of Congress.

This mixed set of findings leaves open the possibility that people like democratic processes as defined but that they dislike the particular manifestation of those processes currently characterizing the American political system (the Washington system). But it is our reading that people do not like to see democratic procedures of any stripe, that they do not like long debates, visible compromises, and a deliberate pace. It is certainly true that people want to try democracy without professionalized politicians and without active, visible, professionalized interest-group representation, but they also want to try democracy without the visible democratic procedures themselves.

The people see no inconsistency in such a position. Many are of the belief that we can have a democracy without uncertainty, conflicting options, confusion, bargaining, or compromises for solutions. The lack of realism in this belief makes it hard to accept fully the public's reform agenda. It is our belief that even if abuses of the Washington system could be minimized via reform (and they should be), large portions of the public would still be dissatisfied. They would still be seeing things they did not like because many of these "things" are rooted in the diverse interests and perspectives of the American people. So, for a variety of reasons, reform alone will not do the trick, and we must entertain other possible ways of improving the image of Congress.

Changing congressional policies

If procedural changes will not suffice, perhaps policy changes will. Much popular commentary prior to 1995 was based on the belief that public unrest with Congress was actually the dissatisfaction of conservatives with the membership composition and perceived policy orientation of Congress during the previous decades. In reality, the unrest was much broader than that: 64 percent of Democrats did not approve of Congress, and a similar figure obtained for self-professed liberals. We predict that analysis subsequent to the 1995 reversal in majority parties will likewise highlight a significant percentage of Republicans and conservatives still withholding support for Congress. So even the groups toward which Congress may tilt are anything but enamored with the body. Moreover, Congress is only slightly more distant from the people in perceived ideological terms than the other two branches. The actual difference in perceived distance is minimal and insignificant. What happened to the Democrats in Congress in 1994 is that, in the public mind, they were attached to the disliked processes in government. This, more than perceived policy failures, led to the startling Republican victories in the midterm election.

But the more basic point is that people seldom think in liberal/conservative terms on policy issues. Their main policy complaint with Congress is that it is not solving society's problems, not that it is too far to the left or too far to the right. While it is true that the image of Congress would be greatly enhanced if all of society's problems were eliminated, this is not the same as saying that Congress is unpopular because of its location on the ideological spectrum. Neither is it a very helpful or realistic prescription for how Congress can resurrect its image with the people.

Educating the people about Congress

Yet another popular solution involves giving the people more information about Congress. Like the previous solutions, this one does not withstand analysis. It is tempting for members of Congress and for others close to the institution to maintain that "if the people only knew more about Congress, they would support it." Unfortunately, this is simply not true. While many Americans' views of Congress are factually inaccurate, these inaccuracies often work to favor Congress. People think Congress has 40 percent of the personal staffers it actually has, they think the salary is 75 percent of what it is, and they think members stay only 75 percent as long as they do. If people were better schooled about the pension plan, perquisite package, salaries, staff, and length of service, their feelings toward Congress would not improve. They would quite likely worsen.

Consider term limits. When we apprised term-limit opponents of the common arguments in favor of the reform, and when we apprised term-limit advocates of the common arguments against it, the opponents were the ones who changed their minds. Very few supporters of term limits were swayed by new information, while more than 40 percent of the term-limit opponents were. In this case and, we suspect, many others, people's lack of basic factual information, and their unfamiliarity with the arguments on the issues, are not the main problems. Just because the level of knowledge and debate concerning Congress may not be what we think it should be does not mean an improvement in these levels would make attitudes more positive.

This line of thought is buttressed by the more general finding that educational attainment is not positively related to approval of Congress. Though it is instructive to note that approval of the *institution* of Congress increases with education, approval of the *members* of Congress does not. For many groups, notably Republicans and Independents in 1992, it even appears as though education and approval of the congressional membership is negatively related. Often, the more that people pay attention to the news and are involved with politics, the more they expect and the more they know about actual events, many of which are negative. So the solution to Congress's dismal public standing is not to be found in additional education of the usual variety.

Educating the people about modern democracy

The real failure of the American people is not that they are unable to recall the name of the secretary of state, that they do not know how many senators represent each state, or that they think Judge Wapner is the chief justice of the Supreme Court. It is not that they are unaware of the steps by which a bill becomes a law. It is not even that they vote too infrequently and use superficial criteria when they do, as many observers contend.

No, citizens' big failure is that they lack an appreciation for the ugliness of democracy. And no wonder. Politicians are not anxious to tell them. Who runs for office by emphasizing his ability to bargain and compromise? Who runs by saying that the problems are really difficult and that true solutions are probably nonexistent? Who runs by saying she is going to emphasize debate and deliberation? Who runs by emphasizing the extent to which the public is divided on key issues?

Blame should not be restricted to politicians. Those of us involved in formal education apparently have not been doing a good job describing the public-relations problems facing open democracies. No correlation seems to exist between years of schooling and a willingness to appreciate the importance of debate and compromise. Developing this appreciation is something that should be a standard part of the educational experience in a democracy, but apparently is not.

Scholars have done much research on the extent to which the mass public as well as political elites are committed to "democratic values" (see, for example, Stouffer, 1955). It is interesting to note that in these studies democratic values are defined as support for civil liberties. But this conceptualization does not go nearly far enough. People, for example, could be willing to allow a communist to speak at their children's school but could still be uncommitted to the broader notions of democratic procedures we are emphasizing. Are people really committed to democracy's "open canvass of ideas"? Are they willing to recognize that reasonable people disagree on tough issues and that working through these problems in a truly democratic fashion will be tortuous, contentious, and time-consuming?

In truth, the American people are quite committed to the rules of the democratic game; the problem is that they are not committed to the game itself. When reading the rule book they often say, "This is wonderful, don't change a thing." When observing the game in action they say, "This is terrible, something must be done." Just providing information on government or on Congress will not solve the problem. Instead, we must attempt to communicate to as many people as possible that democratic processes are not naturally endearing.

And various features of the modern world worsen the situation for governing institutions. Technology and the media's eagerness to report any and all events make it possible for citizens to view democratic processes with all blemishes revealed. In addition, modernity adds professionalized bells and special-interest whistles to standard democratic procedures. As we have already noted, these features are extremely unpopular with the vast majority of citizens, who yearn for simple government and visibly equitable representation. All this combines to put government under greater pressure today than ever before.

THEORIZING ABOUT SUPPORT FOR POLITICAL INSTITUTIONS

Much has been written about the tenuous position of the Supreme Court in our political system. Without its own enforcement capability and without clear accountability of the sort enjoyed by other institutions, it is often thought to be, in the words of Caldeira and Gibson, "an uncommonly vulnerable institution" (1992: 635). Similarly, much has been written about the incredible expectations people place upon the president. The performance, we are told, could never match expectations, thereby guaranteeing public disappointment and disaffection (Barger, 1984).

While not wishing to deny that the Supreme Court is vulnerable and the presidency demanding, our research on public attitudes and political institutions makes it clear that Congress is easily the most vulnerable institution. It is structured to embody what we dislike about modern democratic government, which is almost everything. Because it is so public, Congress's professionalization and association with interest-group representatives is all the more obvious. The Supreme Court may be a "counter-majoritarian institution," that is, an institution that at times adopts policy positions knowingly opposed to the wishes of the popular majority (see Casper, 1976, and Dahl, 1957, for different views on this point). But the more telling factor for ordinary people is *process*, and in terms of process, Congress is clearly the counter-majoritarian institution. It is the institution at odds with what the people want to see procedurally.

These views have implications for our understanding of institutions outside the United States. Our basic contention is that, other things being equal, the more a meaningful political institution publicly displays modern democratic procedures, the less public approval that institution will be accorded. If true, this contention stands on its head much of what has been written about legislative bodies, American and otherwise. Since most national legislatures do not perform serious lawmaking work, and are therefore commonly called parliaments rather than legislatures, it was sensible for earlier research to ask what function or functions they perform. The most pervasive answer provided in the literature was that they contribute to the granting of public support and legitimacy to the political systems. Citizens feel better about their government knowing there is a legislative body involved (see Loewenberg, 1971; Packenham, 1970; Wahlke, 1971).

The trouble is, the evidence for this position was never real. The phantom conclusion was based primarily on the logic that since legislatures existed in so many systems they must do something. Was it not likely that this "something" was to boost system support and legitimacy by bringing the government closer to the people? We contend that this logic is wrong. We believe that legislatures not only fail to contribute to popular support for a political system, but diminish this support. In this sense, the strategy of hiding legislatures amid the executive and majority coalition in a type of parliamentary as opposed to presidential system is a wise one, although we are speaking here only in terms of the effects of system type on public support, not about the overall ability of the legislature to contribute to the governing process.

But if legislatures are so damaging to public support for the political system, why stop with camouflaging them? Why not do away with legislatures and their unavoidable bad-guy status? The answer is that deep down there is most definitely value in having a legislature as part of a political system, but this value is easy to miss. Easton was right that there are different types of support. But he was wrong to stress the distinction between diffuse and specific support. For Easton, the key characteristic of support is what it takes to change its level. With specific support, it takes very little. If an unfavorable output is replaced by a favorable one, people may suddenly display support where they did not before. With diffuse support, outputs by definition do not alter levels of support.

We argue that the crucial distinction actually has to do not with how support can be altered, but with the nature of the support itself. People are not supportive of legislatures in an *operational* sense – the day-to-day attitudes we have analyzed at length in this book. But people do recognize at a more *existential* level that a system without a legislature would be dangerously flawed. For all their negativity toward legislatures, people the world over, including those in the United States, do not want their legislatures to be disbanded (see also Mishler & Rose, 1993).[2] They believe the absence of a legislature would be dangerous.

Thus, there may be little cause for alarm. Perhaps we need not worry about the American people's tendency to deny Congress operational support as long as they continue to afford it existential support. The public certainly acts as though it can visit daily blows upon Congress without endangering the long-term viability of the institution itself. In a sense, this is true. Congress is not going to go away as a result of public disrespect. But the jabs and punches leave their mark. The lack of operational support renders Congress vulnerable to structural reform proposals that may or may not improve the body. It also causes laws passed by Congress to be imbued with decidedly less sanctity (witness the broad public support for Oliver North's belief that he could act in violation of the Boland Amendment as long as he felt this action was for the good of the country). Moreover, it discourages quality people from seeking to become members, and it contributes mightily to public cynicism about the entire political process. In short, the pervasive lack of operational public support for Congress cannot be waved off. It matters, and as we have just seen, improving operational support is not something that can be achieved easily.

It may be comforting to note that people recognize that the absence of Congress would be bad; but Congress is in need of people who are willing to believe that its presence is good. To achieve this, we advocate a two-pronged strategy. First, the public's distaste for the core features of any real-life democracy – disagreement, debate, compromise, all probably at a measured pace – must be addressed by a totally restructured educational process. Schooling on constitutional and institutional niceties desperately needs to be accompanied by schooling on unavoidable democratic realities. From the start, teachers need to expose children to the extent to which Americans disagree with each other on most matters. This being established, teachers should teach children to see that the only democratic way to handle these disagreements is by airing our differ-

2 We pretested a question on the desire to get rid of Congress and there was so little support for the proposal that we did not include the item in our final survey instrument. People would object, possibly with dire consequences, if laws were made in a high-handed fashion by an executive alone (for an interesting account of the pros and cons of legislative involvement in lawmaking, see Alexander, 1993).

ences, by debating various proposals, and, almost certainly, by compromising for the sake of arriving at some solution. If we fail to teach the American public that debate and compromise are not synonymous with bickering and selling out, operational support will never be forthcoming.

But the public's lack of appreciation for what we have been calling the messiness inherent in democratic processes is not the only problem. This is why we are proposing a second part to the strategy for improving operational support of Congress. The public is especially upset by the particular kinds of democratic procedures present in the modern Congress. David Mayhew once wrote that we would be "hard pressed" to design a Congress that better served "members' electoral needs" than the one he was looking at in the mid-1970s (1974: 82). It could be added that we would be equally hard-pressed to design a Congress that less accurately reflected the process preferences of the people than the one we see in the mid-1990s.

The elaborate institutional infrastructure, the committees, the subcommittees, the staffers, the partisanship, the nature of debate, the puffery, the boundaries, the sense of insularity, the lengthy careers, the perquisites, the salary, the maldistributed pork, and the special-interest representatives attracted to Congress like bees to honey all serve as tremendous turn-offs for large portions of the citizenry. It is essential that the country conduct an informed debate on the modern manifestation of Congress. Do we need the current level of professionalization? Will Congress collapse in the face of a marked reduction in salaries, staffers, or terms of service? Is there some way to improve the people's perceptions of interest groups interacting with members of Congress? Could the way Congress currently represents interests be improved via campaign-finance reforms, further gift-giving restrictions, and other more imaginative ways of involving ordinary people? (See Broder, 1994.)

By raising these questions, we are not implying that the answers are automatically yes. But to date debate on these matters has been disappointing. Institutional insiders have been unbending and either oblivious to, or unwilling to consider, the consequences of perpetuating the status quo for public attitudes toward the institution. The public, on the other hand, often adopts a knee-jerk populist agenda that is based on the ostrich-style belief that society has not changed since Jefferson's time. Somewhere between those who never met a perquisite or additional staffer they did not like, and those who think Cincinnatus is still alive, resides the truth. If by scholarly research and public debate we can come to an improved understanding of the extent to which professionalization is or is not necessary in a developed society with an activist governmental sector, and if we can come to an improved understanding of how the process of representing interests is likely to be modified by the simple fact that the society now has nearly 300 million people and a plethora of interests, then we will be better able to construct an appropriate battery of reforms. Only when an activist yet realistic reform agenda is combined with people who recognize the inevitably unruly nature of all democratic processes, will we be in a position to expect much in the way of improvement in public attitudes concerning the political entity most burdened by its open embodiment of these processes.

Appendix

NATIONAL SURVEY

The data sets used throughout most of this book are part of the Perceptions of Congress project funded by the National Science Foundation. The telephone-survey data were collected by the Bureau of Sociological Research at the University of Nebraska, Lincoln. The bureau hired and trained interviewers for this project. The bureau purchased a list of telephone numbers from a national random sample and then randomly generated the last digit of the telephone number. When interviewers called a household, they asked to speak to the person in the household who was at least 18 years old and who had had the most recent birthday (Salmon & Nichols, 1983). The telephone interviews were conducted from July to October 1992 and had a 57 percent response rate. A total of 1,433 people completed the survey.

The survey items and scales used in the regression analyses in Chapters 6 and 7 were standardized to range from 0 to 1, making comparisons across variables easier. See King (1986) and Luskin (1991) for a discussion of how to interpret scales using this method of standardizing variables.

Demographics

Education: What is the highest level of education you have completed? 1 = less than high school; 2 = some high school; 3 = high school graduate; 4 = some technical school; 5 = technical school graduate; 6 = some college; 7 = college graduate; 8 = postgraduate or professional degree.

Education categories: 1 through 3 = low education; 4 through 6 = middle education; 7, 8 = high education.

Income: Was your total household income in 1991 above or below $35,000? 1 = above; 2 = below. [Respondents were then asked:] I am going to mention a number of income categories. When I come to the category that describes your total household income before taxes in 1991, please stop me.

Income scale: 1 = under 5 thousand; 2 = 5 to 10 thousand; 3 = 10 to 15 thousand; 4 = 15 to 20 thousand; 5 = 20 to 25 thousand; 6 = 25 to 30 thousand; 7 = 30 to 35 thousand; 8 = 35 to 40 thousand; 9 = 40 to 50 thousand; 10 = 50 to 60 thousand; 11 = 60 to 70 thousand; 12 = 70 to 100 thousand; 13 = 100 thousand or more.

Income categories: 1 through 5 = low income; 6 through 9 = middle income; 10 through 13 = high income.

Race: What race do you consider yourself? 1 = white/Caucasian; 2 = Mexican/hispanic; 3 = black/African-American; 4 = American Indian/Native American; 5 = Oriental/Asian; 6 = other.

Race categories: 1 = whites; 2 through 5 = people of color.

Age: In what year were you born?

Political attitudes

Party identification: Generally speaking, do you usually think of yourself as a Democrat, a Republican, an Independent, or something else?

[If Democrat/Republican] Would you call yourself a strong Democrat/Republican or not a very strong Democrat/Republican? 1 = strong; 2 = not very strong.

[If Independent] Do you think of yourself as closer to the Republican or Democratic party? 1 = Democratic; 2 = Republican; 3 = neither; 4 = other.

Party-identification scale: 1 = Strong Democrat; 2 = Weak Democrat; 3 = Independent leaning Democratic; 4 = Independent; 5 = Independent leaning Republican; 6 = Weak Republican; 7 = Strong Republican.

External Efficacy: Possible responses 0 = agree; 1 = disagree (coefficient alpha .52).

> People like me don't have any say about what the government does.
> I don't think public officials care much about what people like me think.
>
> External efficacy scale: low efficacy = 0 to high efficacy = 2.

Ideology: Possible responses 1 = liberal; 2 = slightly liberal; 3 = moderate; 4 = slightly conservative; 5 = conservative.

Appendix

Self – We hear a lot of talk these days about liberals and conservatives. Do you consider yourself liberal, slightly liberal, moderate, slightly conservative, or conservative?

Congress – What about Congress?

President – What about George Bush?

Supreme Court – What about the Supreme Court?

Ideological differences: 0 = no ideological difference to 4 = extreme ideological difference.

Absolute Value (Self–Congress); Absolute Value (Self–president); Absolute Value (Self–Supreme Court).

Political Involvement: Additive scale of three variables (interest, discuss politics, vote): 0 = low involvement to 6 = high involvement (coefficient alpha .64).

Interest: How interested are you in politics and national affairs? Are you very interested, somewhat interested, slightly interested, or not at all interested? 1 = not at all interested; 2 = slightly interested; 3 = somewhat interested; 4 = very interested. Recoded 1,2 = 0; 3 = 1; 4 = 2.

Discuss Politics: How many days in the past week did you talk about politics with your family or friends? 0 days to 7 days. Recoded 0,1 = 0; 2 through 5 = 1; 6,7 = 2.

Vote: In 1988 George Bush ran on the Republican ticket against Michael Dukakis for the Democrats. Do you remember for sure whether or not you voted in that election? In 1990 elections were held for the U.S. House of Representatives. Do you remember for sure whether or not you voted in that election? 0 = no, didn't vote/doesn't think so; 1 = yes, did vote/thinks so. Coded 0 = did not vote in either; 1 = voted in one of the two elections; 2 = voted in both elections.

Contact representative: Have you or anyone in your household ever contacted your representative in the U.S. House of Representatives or anyone in his or her office? 0 = no; 1 = yes.

Expertise: I'm going to ask you some questions about government. Most people aren't sure of the correct answer, but we are interested in their best guesses. If you aren't sure of the answer, please make a guess.

Can you recall who is head of the new Russian republic?

Do you happen to recall who is the secretary of state?

Who is the secretary of defense?

Is the current federal budget deficit larger or smaller than it was when Ronald Reagan first took office in 1981?

Appendix

Expertise categories: (all answers coded o = wrong, 1 = correct) 0,1 = novice; 2,3 = middle category; 4 = expert.

Evaluations

Open-ended like/dislike questions: Up to three answers were coded for each of the four questions.

Federal Government: Many people have been talking about the federal government lately. Please think about some good and bad points of the federal government. Is there anything you like about the federal government? Is there anything you dislike about the federal government?

Congress: Many people have been talking about the U.S. Congress lately. Please think about some good and bad points of Congress. Is there anything you like about Congress? Is there anything you dislike about Congress?

Approval ratings: Possible responses for all questions were 1 = strongly disapprove; 2 = disapprove; 3 = approve; 4 = strongly approve.

Institutions: I have a few more questions about the institutions of the government in Washington – that is, the presidency, the Supreme Court, and Congress. In general, do you strongly approve, approve, disapprove, or strongly disapprove of the institution of the presidency, no matter who is in office? What about the Supreme Court, no matter who the justices are? What about the U.S. Congress, no matter who is in office?

Members of institutions: Again, thinking about people in government, please tell me if you strongly approve, approve, disapprove, or strongly disapprove of the way the people are handling their jobs. How do you feel about the way the nine justices on the Supreme Court have been handling their job? What about President George Bush? What about the 535 members of Congress? What about the leaders of Congress? What about your own representative in the U.S. House of Representatives?

Feeling Thermometers: Responses for all questions ranged from o (very cold) to 100 (very warm).

Members of institutions: I'd like to get your feelings toward some groups of people in the U.S. government. I'll read the name of a group and I'd like you to rate it using something we call the feeling thermometer. Ratings between 50 and 100 degrees mean that you feel favorable and warm toward that group. Ratings between o and 50 degrees mean that you don't feel favorable toward the group and that you don't care too much for that group. You would rate the group at the 50-degree mark if you don't feel particularly warm or cold toward the group. Using the feeling thermometer, how would you rate the justices currently serving on the U.S. Supreme Court? How would you rate the current president, George Bush? How would you rate the current members of Congress?

Institutions: Now, I've asked you to rate some people in government, but sometimes when we talk about the parts of the government in Washington, like the Supreme Court, the presidency, and the Congress, we don't mean the people currently serving in office, we mean the institutions themselves, no matter who's in office. These institutions have their own buildings, historical traditions, and purposes laid out in the Constitution. I'd like to know how warm or cold you feel toward these institutions, not the people currently in office. Using the feeling thermometer, how would you rate the U.S. Supreme Court? How would you rate the presidency? How would you rate the U.S. Congress as an institution?

Emotions: Now I'd like to have you compare your feelings toward people in government – the Supreme Court justices, the president, and members of Congress. Which makes you feel the most angry – the Supreme Court justices, the president, or members of Congress? Which makes you feel most afraid? Which makes you feel most disgusted? Which makes you feel most uneasy? And which makes you feel most proud?

Power: All responses were coded 1 = not enough power; 2 = about the right amount of power; 3 = too much power.

The institutions of government in Washington, no matter who is in office, need a certain amount of power for the good of the country and the individual person. Please tell me if the institution has too much power, not enough power, or about the right amount of power. The U.S. Supreme Court? What about the presidency? What about the U.S. Congress?

Most important problem: What do you think is the single most important problem facing this country? [Open-ended question] How good a job is the U.S. Congress doing in dealing with this problem, a good job, a fair job, or a poor job? How good a job is the president doing in dealing with this problem, a good, fair, or poor job? How good a job is the U.S. Supreme Court doing in dealing with this problem, a good, fair, or poor job? 1 = poor job; 2 = fair job; 3 = good job.

Congress Questions

Important jobs of representatives: Possible responses to all questions coded 1 = not important; 2 = somewhat important; 3 = very important.

Now I would like to know what you think is the most important part of a representative's job. I'll read you several jobs that members of the House of Representatives do. Please tell me whether you think the job is very important, somewhat important, or not important.

Stopping the president from getting too much power

Helping the people in their district deal with the government bureaucracy

Bringing federal dollars and projects, such as military bases and dams, back to the district

Passing laws on important national problems

Discussing and debating controversial issues

Compromising with the president

Congress statements: Possible responses were 1 = strongly disagree; 2 = disagree; 3 = neutral; 4 = agree; 5 = strongly agree. We reversed coding where necessary so that pro-Congress responses were assigned higher numbers.

Congress does a good job representing the diverse interests of Americans, whether black or white, rich or poor.

Congress addresses difficult issues in a reasonably efficient way.

Congress is too far removed from ordinary people. (reversed)

Congress is too heavily influenced by interest groups when making decisions. (reversed)

There are too many staffers or assistants in Congress. (reversed)

Members of Congress should do what their district wants them to do even if they think it is a bad idea.

Just a few members of Congress have all the power. (reversed)

Members of Congress focus too much on events in Washington. (reversed)

Members of Congress come back to their districts too often.

Members of Congress should do what is best for the entire country, not just their district.

Members of Congress are too sensitive to what the public opinion polls tell them their constituents want. (reversed)

Events: Many people are complaining lately about the people who serve in Congress. Others think the members of Congress are doing a fine job. What about you? Are you satisfied or dissatisfied with the members of Congress in recent years? 1 = dissatisfied; 2 = both dissatisfied and satisfied; 3 = satisfied.

[If dissatisfied] There are many reasons why people might have negative feelings toward Congress. I would like to know how much each of the following actions of Congress contribute to your negative feelings. Did the action contribute a great deal, some, a little, or not at all to your feelings? 1 = not at all; 2 = a little; 3 = some; 4 = a great deal.

> Members of Congress voting for their own pay raise
> The Clarence Thomas–Anita Hill hearings
> The overdrafts at the House bank
> Gridlock over the budget deficit

Reforms: Possible responses were favor or oppose.

Some people have suggested that we need to reform some aspects of government. Others think we ought to leave things the way they are. I am going to read you some proposed reforms. Please tell me whether you favor or oppose each reform. If you aren't sure, just say you don't know. If you want the reform explained, please let me know. 1 = favor; 2 = oppose.

> Lengthening the term served by members of the U.S. House of Representatives, say from two years to four years
> Requiring that the federal budget be balanced
> Reducing the salary for members of Congress

Term limits: Limiting the number of terms someone can serve in Congress.

[If favor] Would you say you strongly favor or not very strongly favor term limitations?

Some people opposed to term limitations have suggested that the problems Congress deals with are so complex that it takes years for members of Congress to develop the expertise needed to address those problems. Have you thought at all about this argument? [Yes or No] Being aware of this argument, would you still favor limiting the number of terms someone can serve in Congress? [Yes or No]

Other people opposed to term limitations have suggested that limiting terms for members of Congress would only increase the power of unelected staff members and interest-group lobbyists. Have you thought at all about this argument? [Yes or No] Being aware of this argument, would you still favor limiting the number of terms someone can serve in Congress? [Yes or No]

[If oppose] Would you say you strongly oppose or not very strongly oppose term limitations?

Some people in favor of term limitations are concerned that current members of Congress, who win better than 95 percent of the time, don't give other people the chance to get into office. Have you thought at all about this argument? [Yes or No] Being aware of this argument, would you still oppose limiting the number of terms someone can serve in Congress? [Yes or No]

Other people in favor of term limitations have suggested that the longer representatives are in Congress the more they are influenced by the Washington interest-group scene. Have you thought at all about this argument? [Yes or No] Being aware of this argument, would you still oppose limiting the number of terms someone can serve in Congress? [Yes or No]

Facts about Congress: Now I'm going to ask you some questions about Congress. Again, most people aren't sure of the correct answers, but we are interested in their best guesses. If you aren't sure of the answer, please make a guess.

> How long is the term of office for a United States senator?
> How many U.S. senators are there from your state?
> Which party, the Republicans or Democrats, has the most members in the U.S. House of Representatives?
> Which party, the Republicans or Democrats, has the most members in the U.S. Senate?
> What is the current salary of members of Congress?
> On average, how many assistants or staff members does each member of the House of Representatives have?
> On average, how many years have the current members of the House of Representatives been in office?

Democratic processes: All of the following are additive scales, with larger scores reflecting more positive attitudes toward democratic procedures, professionalization, and representation.

Democratic procedures: Possible responses to all questions coded 1 = not important; 2 = somewhat important; 3 = very important. Higher scores reflect prodemocratic procedure responses.

Now I would like to know what you think is the most important part of a representative's job. I'll read you several jobs that members of the House of Representatives do. Please tell me whether you think the job is very important, somewhat important, or not important. Discussing and debating controversial issues. . . . Compromising with the President.

Professionalization: Possible responses were 1 = strongly disagree; 2 = disagree; 3 = neutral; 4 = agree; 5 = strongly agree. We reversed coding where necessary so that pro-professionalization responses were assigned higher numbers.

Congress addresses difficult issues in a reasonably efficient way.
There are too many staffers or assistants in Congress. (reversed)
Just a few members of Congress have all the power. (reversed)
Members of Congress focus too much on events in Washington.
  (reversed)

Representation: Possible responses were 1 = strongly disagree;
2 = disagree; 3 = neutral; 4 = agree; 5 = strongly agree. We reversed
coding where necessary so that prorepresentation responses were assigned higher numbers.

Congress does a good job representing the diverse interests of Americans, whether black or white, rich or poor.
Congress is too far removed from ordinary people. (reversed)
Congress is too heavily influenced by interest groups when making
  decisions. (reversed)

FOCUS GROUPS

The focus groups were conducted in two communities in each of four
parts of the country: southeast Nebraska, the Minneapolis–St. Paul area,
Houston, and upstate New York. The eight locations varied in terms of
socioeconomic status, population size of the community, and minority
makeup of the community. For example, we conducted one focus-group
session in a heavily Native American section of Minneapolis and one in
a relatively wealthy suburb of St. Paul.

The focus groups included from six to twelve people and lasted about
two hours. Participants were promised and received $20 ($25 in Houston) for their involvement. Focus-group participants were contacted by
various means, including posting announcements in public places, plac-
ing announcements on car windows in parking lots, calling people at
random in a community telephone directory, asking people at public
events to make an announcement about the study, hiring a professional
organization to enlist volunteers, and, when necessary, asking people on
the street to be a part of the study. Although the focus-group participants
were not a random sample, they did vary in age, race, socioeconomic
status, and political leanings. Interested readers may contact the authors
for a more detailed description of the focus-group participants (see also
Krueger, 1988; Morgan, 1988; Stewart & Shamdasani, 1990).

The moderator worked from a list of prepared questions. Deviations
from the order of the list were common, although all of the questions
were asked at some point in all of the focus groups. The focus-group
question protocol follows:

Appendix

Focus-group questions

1. As a way to get started, let's talk about your feelings toward the national government. What are the most important things the president, the Supreme Court, and Congress should be doing now and are they doing these things?

(Probe if necessary: What about the president? What about the Supreme Court? What about the Congress?)

Follow-up: Which branch do you think is the most powerful? The least powerful? Why? Does it depend on the issue?

2. It seems as if people's dissatisfaction with government is heavily focused on Congress lately. What do you think? Are you dissatisfied specifically with Congress or are you more broadly dissatisfied with the national government?

3. Let's discuss Congress now. Ideally we can think of legislatures playing a bunch of different roles, such as passing laws, helping people deal with the bureaucracy, compromising with the president and so on. What do you think is the primary role the U.S. Congress plays today? What kinds of things does Congress do?

Probe: What do you expect from Congress? What could Congress do if it were working really well? What's gone wrong? That is, why isn't Congress doing what we expect from it? Have you been upset about Congress for a long time or is this a recent thing? If more recent, what made these negative feelings come about?

Follow-up: What changes are needed to improve Congress? That is, what specific reforms would make Congress better deliver what we want from it? (E.g., term limitations, lengthening the terms of representatives, having a balanced-budget amendment, etc.) What is it about these changes that would do the trick?

4. Now I'd like to shift away from focusing on Congress and talk about citizens themselves. As we've discussed, there are problems with Congress and the government that people seem pretty upset about. Part of the blame for what's gone wrong obviously falls on the politicians and people in Washington, but what about the citizens? What should citizens be doing that they aren't?

Probe: Should citizens be actively involved in politics or should we be able to leave it up to our representatives to take care of these matters?

Probe: What should we expect from our representatives given our own duties as citizens?

Follow-up: Some people think members of Congress are out of touch with the people in their districts, while others think Congress members are in a sense *too* in touch, that is, they are too eager to follow opinion polls rather than lead. What do you think? What should the relationship be between representatives and citizens?

Probe: Who do you think does a better job representing your interests: Congress as a whole, your own representative, or the president?

Probe: Do we need strong national institutions or would it be best if people could govern themselves?

An assistant tape recorded the sessions and kept track of participants' comments with pen and paper. The tape recordings were later transcribed. We analyzed the transcripts systematically, first by examining the connections people made among various political objects (for example, if people began talking about the presidency and then shifted to a specific discussion of then-president Bush, we noted the connection) and then by organizing the comments topically (for example, under the topic "Supreme Court" we looked separately at comments on the institution and then on the justices). Using this method, we were able to examine both the quantity of comments and evaluations made about certain institutions or members and the linkages among various attitudes.

References

Adorno, T. W., E. Frenkel-Brunswik, D. J. Levinson, and R. N. Sanford. 1950. *The Authoritarian Personality*. New York: Harper & Row.

Ahuja, Sunil, Staci Beavers, Cynthia Berreau, Anthony Dodson, Patrick Hourigan, Steven Showalter, Jeff Walz, and John R. Hibbing. 1994. "Modern Congressional Election Theory Meets the 1992 House Elections." *Political Research Quarterly* 47: 909–921.

Alexander, Gerard. 1993. "Parliament and the Failure of Land Reform in Spain." Paper presented at the Conference on Legislatures and Parliaments in Democratizing and Newly Democratic Regimes, Paris, France, May 1993.

Almond, Gabriel A., and Sidney Verba. 1963. *The Civic Culture*. Princeton, NJ: Princeton University Press.

Altemeyer, Bob. 1988. *Enemies of Freedom: Understanding Right-Wing Authoritarianism*. San Francisco: Jossey-Bass.

American Enterprise Institute/Brookings Institution. 1992. *Renewing Congress: A First Report*. Washington, DC: American Enterprise Institute/Brookings Institution.

Asher, Herbert B. 1976. *Causal Modeling*. Beverly Hills, CA: Sage.

Asher, Herbert B., and Mike Barr. 1993. "Popular Support for Congress and Its Members." Paper presented at the Conference on Congress, the Press, and the Public, Washington, DC, May 1993.

Baas, Larry R. 1980. "The Constitution as Symbol: Patterns of Meaning." *American Politics Quarterly* 8: 237–256.

Balz, Dan, and Richard Morin. 1991. "An Electorate Ready to Revolt." *Washington Post National Weekly Edition*, 11–17 November: 6–7.

Barger, Harold M. 1984. *The Impossible Presidency*. Glenview, IL: Foresman.

Bond, Jon R., Richard Fleisher, and Michael Northrup. 1988. "Public Opinion and Presidential Support." *Annals* 499 (September): 47–63.

Born, Richard. 1990. "The Shared Fortunes of Congress and Congressmen." *Journal of Politics* (November): 1223–1241.

Bowman, Karlyn, and Everett Ladd. 1992. "Public Opinion Toward Congress: An Historical Look." Unpublished paper, American Enterprise Institute, Washington, DC.

Briand, Michael. 1993. "Where Do We Get Our Ideas? A Reply to Nelson Polsby." *PS* (September): 540–543.

References

Broder, David. 1994. "House Ready for Prime Time." *Lincoln Star*, 6 March: 12.

Broder, David, and Richard Morin. 1994. "Why Americans Hate Congress." *Washington Post National Weekly Edition*, 11–17 July: 6–7.

Brody, Richard. 1986. "Candidate Evaluations and the Vote." In Richard Lau and David Sears, eds., *Political Cognition*. Hillsdale, NJ: Erlbaum.

Broh, C. Anthony. 1973. *Toward a Theory of Issue Voting*. Beverly Hills, CA: Sage.

Caldeira, Gregory A. 1986. "Neither the Purse nor the Sword: Dynamics of Public Confidence in the Supreme Court." *American Political Science Review* 80: 1209–1226.

Caldeira, Gregory A., and James L. Gibson. 1992. "The Etiology of Public Support for the Supreme Court." *American Journal of Political Science* 36 (August): 635–664.

Campbell, Angus, Philip E. Converse, Warren E. Miller, and Donald Stokes. 1960. *The American Voter*. New York: Wiley.

Carmines, Edward G., and James A. Stimson. 1980. "The Two Faces of Issue Voting." *American Political Science Review* 74 (March): 78–91.

Casper, Jonathan. 1976. "The Supreme Court and National Policy Making." *American Political Science Review* 70 (March): 50–63.

Citrin, Jack. 1974. "Comment: The Political Relevance of Trust in Government." *American Political Science Review* 68: 973–988.

Coe, Barbara J., and James H. MacLachlan. 1980. "How Major TV Advertisers Evaluate Commercials." *Journal of Advertising Research* 20 (6): 51–54.

Cohen, Richard. 1992. "Congress in Distress." *National Journal*, 18 January: 118–125.

Conover, Pamela Johnston, Ivor M. Crewe, and Donald D. Searing. 1991. "The Nature of Citizenship in the United States and Great Britain." *Journal of Politics* 53 (August): 800–832.

Conover, Pamela Johnston, and Stanley Feldman. 1986. "Emotional Reactions to the Economy: I'm Mad as Hell and I'm Not Going to Take It Anymore." *American Journal of Political Science* 30 (February): 50–78.

Converse, Philip E. 1964. "The Nature of Belief Systems in Mass Publics." In David E. Apter, ed., *Ideology and Discontent*. New York: Free Press.

Cook, Timothy. 1979. "Legislature vs. Legislator: A Note on the Paradox of Congressional Support." *Legislative Studies Quarterly* 4: 43–61.

Craig, Stephen C. 1993. *The Malevolent Leaders: Popular Discontent in America*. Boulder, CO: Westview.

Crick, Bernard. 1992. *In Defense of Politics*, 4th ed. Chicago: University of Chicago Press.

Dahl, Robert A. 1957. "Decision-Making in a Democracy: The Supreme Court as a National Policy-Maker." *Journal of Public Law* 6 (Fall): 270–280.

Davidson, Roger H., David M. Kovenock, and Michael K. O'Leary. 1968. *Congress in Crisis: Politics and Congressional Reform*. Belmont, CA: Wadsworth.

Davidson, Roger H., and Glenn R. Parker. 1972. "Positive Support for Political Institutions: The Case of Congress." *Western Political Quarterly* 25: 600–612.

Davis, Richard. 1994. *Decisions and Images: The Supreme Court and the Press*. Englewood Cliffs, NJ: Prentice Hall.

Dennis, Jack. 1973. "Public Support for American National Political Institu-

References

tions." Paper presented at the Conference on Public Support for the Political System, August 1973, Madison, WI.

——— 1981. "Public Support for Congress." *Political Behavior* 3: 319–350.

Devine, Donald J. 1972. *The Political Culture of the United States.* Boston: Little, Brown.

Dionne, E. J., Jr. 1991. *Why Americans Hate Politics.* New York: Simon & Schuster.

Dolbeare, Kenneth M., and Phillip E. Hammond. 1968. "The Political Party Basis of Attitudes Toward the Supreme Court." *Public Opinion Quarterly* 37: 16–30.

Duncan, Phil. 1991. "Defending Congress, the Institution." *Congressional Quarterly Weekly Report,* 30 November: 3554.

Durkheim, Emile. 1947. *The Division of Labor in Society.* Glencoe, IL: Free Press.

Durr, Robert H., John B. Gilmour, and Christina Wolbrecht. 1994. "Explaining Congressional Approval." Paper presented at the annual meeting of the American Political Science Association, New York, September 1–4, 1994.

Easton, David. 1965a. *A Framework for Political Analysis.* Englewood Cliffs, NJ: Prentice-Hall.

——— 1965b. *A Systems Analysis of Political Life.* New York: Wiley.

——— 1975. "A Reassessment of the Concept of Political Support." *British Journal of Political Science* 5: 435–457.

——— 1990. *The Analysis of Political Structure.* New York: Routledge.

Ehrenhalt, Alan. 1991. *The United States of Ambition: Politicians, Power, and the Pursuit of Office.* New York: Times Books.

——— 1992. "An Embattled Institution." *Governing* (January): 28–33.

Eisenstadt, S. N. 1964. "Institutionalization and Change." *American Sociology Review* 29: 235–247.

Erber, Ralph, and Richard Lau. 1990. "Political Cynicism Revisited: An Information-Processing Reconciliation of Policy-Based and Incumbency-Based Interpretations of Changes in Trust in Government." *American Journal of Political Science* 34: 236–253.

Farmer, Rick. 1993. "Alienation and Term Limits." Paper presented at the annual meeting of the Southwestern Political Science Association, New Orleans, LA, March 1993.

Fenno, Richard F., Jr. 1975. "If, as Ralph Nader Says, Congress is 'The Broken Branch,' How Come We Love Our Congressmen So Much?" In Norman J. Ornstein, ed., *Congress in Change: Evolution and Reform.* New York: Praeger.

Fiorina, Morris P. 1977. *Congress: Keystone of the Washington Establishment.* New Haven, CT: Yale University Press.

——— 1981. *Retrospective Voting in American National Elections.* New Haven, CT: Yale University Press.

——— 1988. "The Reagan Years: Turning to the Right on Groping toward the Middle." In Barry Cooper, Allan Kornberg, and William Mishler, eds., *The Resurgence of Conservatism in Anglo-American Democracies.* Durham, NC: Duke University Press.

——— 1992. *Divided Government.* New York: Macmillan.

Fund, John H. 1992. "Term Limitation: An Idea Whose Time Has Come." In Gerald Benjamin and Michael J. Malbin, eds., *Limiting Legislative Terms.* Washington: Congressional Quarterly.

References

Gamson, William A. 1968. *Power and Discontent.* Homewood, IL: Dorsey.
    1992. *Talking Politics.* Cambridge University Press.
Gibbs, Nancy. 1990. "Keep the Bums In." *Time,* 19 November: 32–42.
Handberg, Roger. 1984. "Public Opinion and the United States Supreme Court,
    1935–1981." *International Social Science Review* 59: 3–13.
Hanson, Russell L. 1989. "Democracy." In James Farr and Russell L. Hanson,
    eds., *Political Innovation and Conceptual Change.* Cambridge University
    Press.
Harris, Louis. 1987. *Inside America.* New York: Vintage.
Hibbing, John R. 1982. "Voluntary Retirements from the House: The Costs of
    Congressional Service." *Legislative Studies Quarterly* 7 (February): 57–74.
    1991. *Congressional Careers: Contours of Life in the U.S. House of Represen-*
    tatives. Chapel Hill, NC: University of North Carolina Press.
Hibbing, John R., and Samuel C. Patterson. 1994. "Public Attitudes Toward
    the New Parliaments of Central and Eastern Europe." *Political Studies* 42
    (December): 570–592.
Higgenbotham, James B., and Keith K. Cox. 1979. *Focus Group Interviews: A*
    Reader. Chicago, IL: American Marketing Association.
Hook, Janet. 1990. "Incumbents Get the Jitters as Voters Grow Angry." *Con-*
    gressional Quarterly Weekly Report, 4 August: 2473–2477.
Huntington, Samuel P. 1965. "Congressional Responses to the Twentieth Cen-
    tury." In David B. Truman, ed., *Congress and America's Future.* Englewood
    Cliffs, NJ: Prentice-Hall.
Jewell, Malcolm E. 1982. *Representation in State Legislatures.* Lexington: Uni-
    versity of Kentucky Press.
Joint Committee on the Organization of Congress. 1993. *Text of Proceedings.*
    Washington, DC: U.S. Government Printing Office.
Katz, Jeffrey L. 1992. "Record Rate of Retirements Suggests Major Shakeup."
    Congressional Quarterly Weekly Report 50 (4 April): 851–855.
Kernell, Samuel. 1978. "Explaining Presidential Popularity." *American Political*
    Science Review 72: 506–522.
Kessel, John H. 1966. "Public Perceptions of the Supreme Court." *Midwest*
    Journal of Political Science 10: 167–191.
Kettering Foundation. 1991. *Citizens and Politics: A View from Main Street*
    America. Dayton, OH: Kettering Foundation.
King, Anthony. 1992. "Whoever Said the U.S. President Was Powerful?" Paper
    presented at the annual meeting of the American Political Science Associa-
    tion, Chicago, September 1992.
King, Gary. 1986. "How Not to Lie with Statistics." *American Journal of Po-*
    litical Science 39: 666–687.
King, Gary, and Lyn Ragsdale. 1988. *The Elusive Executive.* Washington, DC:
    Congressional Quarterly.
Kirkpatrick, James J. 1992. "Term Limits Notion Has Many Limitations of Its
    Own." *Chicago Sun-Times,* 5 September: 19.
Krueger, Richard. 1988. *Focus Groups: A Practical Guide for Applied Research.*
    Newbury Park, CA: Sage.
Kuklinski, James, Ellen Riggle, Victor Ottati, Norbert Schwarz, and Robert
    Wyer, Jr. 1991. "The Cognitive and Affective Bases of Political Tolerance
    Judgments." *American Journal of Political Science* 35 (February): 1–27.
Ladd, Everett Carll, Jr. 1990. "Public Opinion and the 'Congress Problem.' "
    Public Interest 100: 57–67.

References

Lane, Robert E. 1962. *Political Ideology*. New York: Free Press.

Lau, Richard. 1986. "Political Schemata, Candidate Evaluations, and Voting Behavior." In Richard Lau and David O. Sears, eds., *Political Cognition*. Hillsdale, NJ: Erlbaum.

——— 1989. "Construct Accessibility and Electoral Choice." *Political Behavior* 11: 5–32.

Lind, Michael. 1992. "A Radical Plan to Change American Politics." *Atlantic Monthly* 270 (August): 73–83.

Lipset, Seymour Martin, and William Schneider. 1987. *The Confidence Gap: Business, Labor, and Government in the Public Mind*. Baltimore: Johns Hopkins University Press.

Loewenberg, Gerhard. 1971. "The Role of Parliaments in Modern Political Systems." In Gerhard Loewenberg, ed., *Modern Parliaments: Change or Decline?* Chicago: Aldine.

Luskin, Robert. 1991. "*Abusus non tollit usum*: Standardized Coefficients, Correlations, and R^2s." *American Journal of Political Science* 35: 1032–1046.

McClosky, Herbert. 1964. "Consensus and Ideology in American Politics." *American Political Science Review* 58: 361–382.

McClosky, Herbert, and Alida Brill. 1983. *Dimensions of Tolerance*. New York: Russell Sage Foundation.

McClosky, Herbert, and John Zaller. 1984. *The American Ethos: Public Attitudes Toward Capitalism and Democracy*. Cambridge, MA: Harvard University Press.

McCubbins, Mathew, and Terry Sullivan. 1987. *Congress: Structure and Policy*. Cambridge: Cambridge University Press.

MacKuen, Michael B. 1983. "Political Drama, Economic Conditions, and the Dynamics of Presidential Popularity." *American Journal of Political Science* 27: 165–192.

Madison, James. 1964. "The Senate." In Andrew Hacker, ed., *The Federalist Papers*. New York: Simon & Schuster.

Marcus, George. 1988. "The Structure of Emotional Response: 1984 Presidential Candidates." *American Political Science Review* 82 (September): 737–763.

Marcus, George, and Michael MacKuen. 1993. "Anxiety, Enthusiasm, and the Vote: The Emotional Underpinnings of Learning and Involvement During Presidential Campaigns." *American Political Science Review* 87 (September): 672–685.

Marcus, George, John L. Sullivan, Elizabeth Theiss-Morse, and Sandra Wood. 1995. *With Malice toward Some: How People Make Civil Liberties Judgments*. Cambridge: Cambridge University Press.

Matthews, David. 1991. "After Thoughts." *Kettering Review* (Fall): 78.

Mayhew, David R. 1974. *Congress: The Electoral Connection*. New Haven, CT: Yale University Press.

Miller, Arthur H. 1974. "Political Issues and Trust in Government, 1964–1970." *American Political Science Review* 68: 989–1001.

Miller, Warren E., and Donald E. Stokes. 1963. "Constituency Influence in Congress." *American Political Science Review* 57: 45–56.

Mishler, William, and Richard Rose. 1993. "Public Support for Legislatures and Regimes in Eastern and Central Europe." Paper presented at the Conference on Legislatures and Parliaments in Democratizing and Newly Democratic Regimes, Paris, France, May 1993.

References

Mondak, Jeffery J. 1992. "Institutional Legitimacy, Policy Legitimacy, and the Supreme Court." *American Politics Quarterly* 20 (October): 457–477.

Morgan, David. 1988. *Focus Groups as Qualitative Research*. Newbury Park, CA: Sage.

Morin, Richard. 1995. "Applause Grows for Congress – and for Clinton, Too." *International Herald–Tribune*, 1 February: 3.

Mueller, John E. 1973. *War, Presidents, and Public Opinion*. New York: Wiley.

Murphy, Walter F., and Joseph Tanenhaus. 1968. "Public Opinion and the Supreme Court: The Goldwater Campaign." *Public Opinion Quarterly* 32: 31–50.

Ostrom, Charles W. Jr., and Dennis M. Simon. 1985. "Promise and Performance: A Dynamic Model of Presidential Popularity." *American Political Science Review* 79 (June): 334–358.

Packenham, Robert A. 1970. "Legislatures and Political Development." In Allan Kornberg and Lloyd D. Musolf, eds., *Legislatures in Developmental Perspective*. Durham, NC: Duke University Press.

Page, Benjamin I., and Robert Y. Shapiro. 1992. *The Rational Public: Fifty Years of Trends in Americans' Policy Preferences*. Chicago: University of Chicago Press.

Parker, Glenn R. 1977. "Some Themes in Congressional Unpopularity." *American Journal of Political Science* 21: 93–110.

1981. "Can Congress Ever Be a Popular Institution?" In Joseph Cooper and G. Calvin Mackenzie, eds., *The House at Work*. Austin: University of Texas Press.

Parker, Glenn R., and Roger H. Davidson. 1979. "Why Do Americans Love Their Congressmen So Much More than Their Congress?" *Legislative Studies Quarterly* 4: 52–61.

Patterson, Kelly D., and David B. Magleby. 1992. "The Polls–Poll Trends: Public Support for Congress." *Public Opinion Quarterly* 56: 539–551.

Patterson, Samuel C., and Gregory A. Caldeira. 1990. "Standing Up for Congress: Variations in Public Esteem Since the 1960s." *Legislative Studies Quarterly* 15: 25–47.

Patterson, Samuel C., Ronald D. Hedlund, and G. Robert Boynton. 1975. *Representatives and Represented: Bases of Public Support for the American Legislatures*. New York: Wiley.

Patterson, Samuel C., Randall B. Ripley, and Stephen V. Quinlan. 1992. "Citizens' Orientations Toward Legislatures: Congress and the State Legislature." *Western Political Quarterly* 45 (June): 315–338.

Perry, Duncan M. 1990. "Lukanov's Government Resigns." *Report on Eastern Europe*, 21 December: 1–5.

Polsby, Nelson. 1968. "The Institutionalization of the U.S. House of Representatives." *American Political Science Review* 62: 144–168.

1975. "Goodbye to the Senate's Inner Club." In Norman J. Ornstein, ed., *Congress in Change: Evolution and Reform*. New York: Praeger.

1991. "IGS–Academy Workshop Asks 'What's Wrong with American Political Institutions?' " *Public Affairs Report* 32 (September): 1; 10–12.

1993a. "Where Do You Get Your Ideas?" *PS* 26 (March): 83–87.

1993b. "Response to Michael K. Briand." *PS* 32 (September): 544.

Popkin, Samuel L. 1991. *The Reasoning Voter*. Chicago: University of Chicago Press.

References

Princeton Survey Research Associates. 1994. "Public Attitudes about Campaign Reform." Unpublished manuscript, Princeton, NJ.

Prothro, James, and Charles Grigg. 1960. "Fundamental Principles of Democracy: Bases of Agreement and Disagreement." *Journal of Politics* 22: 276–294.

Public Perspective, The. 1992. "Congress's Ratings at an All-Time Low." 4 (November/December): 86–87.

Rahn, Wendy, John Aldrich, Eugene Borgida, and John Sullivan. 1992. "A Social-Cognitive Model of Candidate Appraisal." In John Ferejohn and James Kuklinski, eds., *Information and Democratic Processes.* Urbana: University of Illinois Press.

Ripley, Randall B., Samuel C. Patterson, Lynn Maurer, and Stephen V. Quinlan. 1992. "Constituents' Evaluations of U.S. House Members." *American Politics Quarterly* 20: 442–456.

Rogowski, Ronald. 1987. "Trade and the Variety of Democratic Institutions." *International Organization* 41 (Spring): 203–223.

Salmon, Charles, and John Spicer Nichols. 1983. "The Next-Birthday Method of Respondent Selection." *Public Opinion Quarterly* 47: 270–276.

Schmidhauser, John R. 1973. "An Exploratory Analysis of the Institutionalization of Legislatures and Judiciaries." In Allan Kornberg, ed., *Legislatures in Comparative Perspective.* New York: McKay.

Schul, Yaacov, and Eugene Burnstein. 1988. "On Greeks and Horses: Impression Formation with Social and Nonsocial Objects." In Thomas Srull and Robert Wyer, Jr., eds., *A Dual Process Model of Impression Formation.* Hillsdale, NJ: Erlbaum.

Seelye, Katharine Q. 1994. "Talks in Congress Reach an Accord to Curb Lobbyists." *New York Times,* 23 September: A1, A9.

Smith, Eric R. A. N. 1989. *The Unchanging American Voter.* Berkeley and Los Angeles: University of California Press.

Social Cognition. 1990. "Thinking About Politics: Comparisons of Experts and Novices" 8 (#1). Guest Editor Jon Krosnick.

Squire, Peverill. 1993. "Professionalization and Public Opinion of State Legislatures." *Journal of Politics* 55 (May): 479–491.

Stewart, David, and Prem Shamdasani. 1990. *Focus Groups: Theory and Practice.* Newbury Park, CA: Sage.

Stimson, James A. 1991. *Public Opinion in America: Moods, Cycles, and Swings.* Boulder, CO: Westview.

Stouffer, Samuel. 1955. *Communism, Conformity, and Civil Liberties.* New York: Doubleday.

Sullivan, Denis, and Roger D. Masters. 1988. " 'Happy Warriors': Leaders' Facial Displays, Viewers' Emotions and Political Support." *American Journal of Political Science* 32 (May): 345–368.

Tanenhaus, Joseph, and Walter F. Murphy. 1981. "Patterns of Public Support for the Supreme Court: A Panel Study." *Journal of Politics* 43: 24–39.

Theiss-Morse, Elizabeth. 1993. "Conceptualizations of Good Citizenship and Political Participation." *Political Behavior* 15: 355–380.

Theiss-Morse, Elizabeth, George Marcus, and John Sullivan. 1993. "Passion and Reason in Political Life: The Organization of Affect and Cognition and Political Tolerance." In George Marcus and Russell Hanson, eds., *Reconsidering the Democratic Public.* University Park: Pennsylvania State University Press.

References

Tyler, Tom. 1990. *Why People Obey the Law*. New Haven, CT: Yale University Press.

Uslaner, Eric. 1992. "Can Reform Change Congress?: The New Institutionalism and Social Engineering." Paper presented at the annual meeting of the American Political Science Association, Chicago, September 1992.

Verba, Sidney, and Norman H. Nie. 1972. *Participation in America: Political Democracy and Social Equality*. New York: Harper & Row.

Wahlke, John C. 1971. "Policy Demands and System Support." *British Journal of Political Science* 1: 271–290.

Weaver, R. Kent, and Bert A. Rockman. 1993. *Do Institutions Matter?* Washington, DC: Brookings Institution.

Weber, Max. 1947. *The Theory of Social and Economic Organization*. Glencoe, IL: Free Press.

Wilentz, Sean. 1993. "Pox Populi: Ross Perot and the Corruption of Populism." *New Republic*, 9 August: 29–35.

Will, George F. 1992. *Restoration: Congress, Term Limits, and the Recovery of Deliberative Democracy*. New York: Free Press.

Wright, James D. 1976. *The Dissent of the Governed: Alienation and Democracy in America*. New York: Academic.

Yankelovich, Daniel. 1991. *Coming to Public Judgment: Making Democracy Work in a Complex World*. Syracuse, NY: Syracuse University Press.

Index

Index